What Do You Do With Joe?

Problem Pupils and Tactful Teachers

written by Elizabeth W. Crisci

STANDARD PUBLISHING
Cincinnati, Ohio

3650

Illustrations by Steve Hayes

Library of Congress Cataloging in Publication Data

Crisci, Elizabeth W.
  What do you do with Joe?

  1. Problem children—Education—Case studies.
  2. Adolescence—Case studies. I. Title.
  LC4801.C63   371.93   81-50236
  ISBN 0-87239-414-X   AACR2

© 1981, The STANDARD PUBLISHING Company, Cincinnati, Ohio
        Division of STANDEX INTERNATIONAL Corporation
Printed in U.S.A.   **3650**

TABLE OF CONTENTS

What Do You Do With Bashful Barb? 5
What Do You Do With Turned-off Terry? 9
What Do You Do With Know-it-all Norm? 13
What Do You Do With Doubting Dick? 17
What Do You Do With Rebellious Rob? 21
What Do You Do With Silly Sarah? 25
What Do You Do With Daydreaming Donna? 29
What Do You Do With Troubled Tom? 33
What Do You Do With Friendless Fran? 37
What Do You Do With Sinful Sam? 41
What Do You Do With Unloved Larry? 45
What Do You Do With Slow-learner Sally? 49
What Do You Do With Domineering Dominick? 53
What Do You Do With Resentful Roger? 57
What Do You Do With Super-spiritual Sharon? 61

CHAPTER ONE
What Do You Do With Bashful Barb?

Bashful Barb is a sweet attractive girl who probably was outgoing and friendly during her earlier growing years. She may be talkative at home, but among her friends and strangers she finds it painful to respond to a question or to carry on a conversation with anyone. Is this from fear of embarrassment, of ridicule, or of showing her ignorance? Why is this pupil so bashful?

Bashful Barb may be self-conscious. If she gives the wrong answers in class, she retires into herself. At some previous time her friends may have laughed at her. She may have been scolded by a parent impatient with her incessant talking. She may have decided it is psychologically safer to be shy, to assume an attractive timidity where she cannot say the wrong words, or be hurt by stupidity. Bashful Barb has consciously chosen to be shy.

Bashful Barb may just be going through a period of change. Growing up may overwhelm her. She retreats from taking responsibility. Forcing a response only adds to her problem. Consider these ways to help her:
  a. Try to understand the agony she is facing.
  b. Give her time to be comfortable in your classroom.
  c. Provide opportunity for voluntary answers or opinions.
  d. Inquire if Barb is a good reader. If she is, ask her to read the Scripture in class.
  e. Let Barb ask the questions (you prepare a list) and more vocal students do the discussing.
  f. Plan ahead. Sudden requests of Barb will frighten and discourage her.
  g. Visit in her home. She may be more comfortable there. Circumstances will help determine this. The telephone is not a good substitute for personal contact.
  h. Ask her to express her ideas in creative writing, possibly through letter writing. This may be easier for her than speaking.
  i. Let the class discuss by twos or threes and choose a spokesman. Barb will not volunteer to speak to the class, but she probably will share in the small group.
  j. Find a common ground of interest and pursue it. Maybe both of you like to sew your own clothes. Accept even a nod or a smile as a reply.

If Barb's bashfulness is a period of change, she will eventually outgrow it. Love and accept her now as she is!

Bashful Barb is really afraid. She may be terrified of others' reaction to her. She expects perfection of herself, and withdraws whenever she fails. Shy people are torn by this dilemma:
- I need people;
- I depend on people;
- I'm afraid of people.

Bashful Barb may feel that if she remains passive, people will like her better. If the class laughs at her wrong answers, you could say, "Thank you for that idea," or "That shows special thought," or "Let's express it this way." If she is ridiculed, she may continue to be afraid to speak. Avoid establishing a "correct answer" attitude. Freedom of speech is essential to good learning. You must be prepared, however, with ideas for a "way out" when uncomfortable situations arise in the classroom. The Scriptures must be the authority for ideas left in the minds of your pupils.

Help Barb overcome her fears and become a part of the group. She must feel at home in your classroom before she can speak her thoughts. Pray that Barb can cope with her shyness. Often it is just a part of growing up.

Bashful Barb may always be shy. If she does not respond after several weeks of the getting-to-know-you treatment, she is not hopeless. God made many different types of people. Maybe Barb will never be an effervescent individual. Her sweet humble spirit may be the means of winning special people. Don't knock it! She is learning, her mind absorbing, her heart opening, and she will find that Christ can put words into her mouth and heal her bashfulness. When the Holy Spirit dwells in her heart, she may want to tell someone.

Be glad that God has made some people quiet. The Bible says, "Study to be quiet" (1 Thessalonians 4:11, 12). The world needs quietness and even a certain measure of shyness in all the noise of modern living.

Let Bashful Barb feel your love and concern while she is one of your pupils. Show her that life is too precious to waste in retreat, then let time do the healing. Rejoice if she emerges from her caterpillar stage of silence into a butterfly stage of participation. Pray that she will learn the joy of knowing and sharing in the love of her heavenly Father, in her own shy, quiet way.

CHAPTER TWO
What Do You Do With Turned-off Terry?

Terry is tall, rugged-looking, with dark, penetrating eyes like his father's. He talks sports, kids around with the girls, and expounds on carburetors and spark plugs. His attendance in class is regular; his peers appreciate his football ability and his casual style.

However, the hour of Bible study shuts him off completely. The young man shows by his lack of interest that he is there only because of family pressure. Terry says religion is for old folks. He wants to have fun and obviously isn't finding it at church. He occupies a seat during the morning hour, but his mind is turned-off from the lesson.

Turned-off Terry can be an exasperation, but he needs your love and attention. He needs answers to important questions. How can you, Teacher, reach Terry?

Is Turned-off Terry hopeless? Are Terry's barriers too thick to be penetrated? No. Many active believers, even Sunday-school teachers and preachers, were once like Turned-off Terry in resisting the gospel. The turned-off pupil may appear in any class, at any age. He can be reached only as the teacher realizes the problem and approaches it prayerfully.

Terry is not an oddball; he is not unique in his response. He has a mind of his own and is going through a phase that requires learning to act without parental pressure to guide him. Because Christianity is a symbol of home, he forces himself to reject it in trying to grow up. He thinks shedding his parents' beliefs and any other authoritative word makes him a "man." His mind has a special resistance to all information that he thinks unnecessary to his life-style.

Along with this cutoff of Christianity, he may wear dirty sox, break the curfew, or skip school. As a duck must learn to swim beyond his mother's protective wing, Terry must learn to live in the big world beyond parental control. The struggle is as hard for the young person as it is for the parent and teacher. Even if God allowed fathers and mothers another opportunity to correct all their mistakes in child rearing, their children would still have certain growing problems! Understanding this helps everyone cope with each problem.

Some children are easy to rear, agreeable with their parents and teachers, maturing early in many aspects of their lives. Others fight the nurturing process all the way. Some may not rebel against their parents' faith, but will struggle against clothing standards, dating suggestions, or doing their share of the chores. Turned-off Terry is combating his parents in a very crucial way involving his soul and eternity.

Teacher, what will you do about Terry?

First, continue teaching the Bible lesson and its application. It is your primary responsibility to teach the Word of God, and your dedication to this principle will be remembered by your students. Because a particular pupil resists, you cannot change the main purpose of the class. You cannot spend the hour showing sport films or playing baseball. God has called you to teach the Bible.

Your commitment must remain true to that goal.

Second, encounter Turned-off Terry by using both verbal and visual illustrations of special interest to him. If you compare Paul's missionary journeys to a football game, Terry will struggle to avoid attention. If you open the class with a Bible baseball game, Terry might participate. If you make flash-card visuals in the shape of hockey sticks, the athletic mind might focus on them. Or tape Bible verses on the outside of a football. Throw the football to the ones who are to read the verses. (A gentle toss is sufficient unless your class is meeting outdoors!) Let the sports-minded student be in charge, preparing the football and planning its use.

Or, each point in the lesson could be a spark plug attached to an "engine" as the lesson progresses. Utilize an old calendar with antique cars by placing discussion questions below each car. Make a vital point with a bag full of auto parts, scrambled together. Unscramble them as the instruction proceeds to exemplify what the gospel does in a life.

The imagination of a creative teacher can open the closed intellect of Turned-off Terry.

Third, involve Terry in the teaching. He can be asked to collect the auto parts and present them one by one during the session. Be specific in what you want. Help wherever possible, but let him take some initiative. He probably knows more about his hobby than you do.

Fourth, spend an afternoon with Turned-off Terry and his buddies, playing football, watching a game he is in, or just talking over a Coke. Show that you care for him and his activities. You must make friends with Terry on his level, not yours. Do not degrade yourself, however, by becoming like him in bad habits, but be complimentary in every area of his acceptable behavior. Visit his home, take time to talk with him before or after church services. Ask about the standing of his team.

It is pretty hard to dislike someone who genuinely likes you. Turned-off Terry will respond under consistent concern from his teacher. He will know if it is false interest.

Fifth, pray for him on a regular basis. Many teachers pray in a general way: "Lord, bless my Sunday-school class." Give the Lord specific requests. He promises to answer in His own time and way. Hardened hearts can melt before the wooing of the Holy Spirit. Classroom atmosphere can turn from cold nothingness to responsive interest after prayer. Turned-off Terry will not be able to resist the Word of God if the Holy Spirit changes his heart, even though a teacher has been exasperated from "trying everything else."

Sixth, go a step further. Seek his help for one of your problems. Terry knows about cars. Ask him to help you discover what that weird noise is in the front end, or let him show you how to change the oil. Ask him to help you get started on a project and he will become an asset in your class. He will realize that you are interested in what he knows. Maybe he will then listen to what you have to say.

To help turned-off Terry you will need to take time:

to continue teaching the Word of God
  using illustrations to cultivate interest
    involving the turned-off pupil in the teaching procedure
      spending time outside the class with him
        praying regularly
          seeking his help on a project.

Turned-off Terry will begin to react favorably to you and eventually to the message. He is your responsibility. Don't be a turned-off teacher in response to him. He is reachable with a little extra effort.

CHAPTER THREE
What Do You Do With Know-it-all Norm?

Know-it-all Norm is a familiar character. There is one in every Sunday-school class! He answers every question before any other student can think or respond. His hand is up or his mouth is open before the last word of a question is uttered. He helps a teacher through difficult periods of uncertainty; he carries you through your lack of preparation, or your fear of silent discussion periods. Know-it-all Norm is missed when he is sick because of the quiet intervals that pervade class discussions.

You can live with Know-it-all Norm, and wait for promotion day. Or, you can face the situation and work for improvement. Know-it-all Norm should learn to respect other opinions and to listen. How will you accomplish this?

First, realize that Know-it-all Norm enjoys monopolizing the class. The teacher is supposed to control a class, but it is possible for one student to usurp that authority and become the center of attention. Do not allow this to happen. The lesson is hindered, sidetracked, and can be lost. A student in control does not allow the teacher time to present the lesson, and it leads other class members to resentment, or laughter. Eventually, Norm has the reputation of a smart aleck, if not checked.

Understanding Norm will help you cope with the situation and find a solution that will not hurt him. You must discover ways to draw out others in the class and give them an equal chance for participation without fear of interruption from Norm. You must learn to prepare a lesson that will overcome the Know-it-all Norm and allow for more uniform participation.

Second, show Know-it-all Norm that he is liked by teacher and class members. He may think that his only recognition is in constant talk, quick answers, and class domination. You must take time to show your love in a tangible way to a student who has more needs than he reveals.

   a. Take him out for a Coke and a talk.
   b. Visit in his home and see his life-style. Perhaps his home is ruled by an unbending father. Norm may never have a chance to voice an opinion; he may be laughed at in his home. His only recognition may be in the classroom. If this is the case, you can show him that God thinks he is important in quiet times as well as in answering all the questions. (1 Thessalonians 4:11; Ecclesiastes 3:7b)

c. Do not allow the class to mock, ridicule, or belittle Norm.
  d. Do not be afraid or put-down by the Know-it-all Norm.
  e. Convey a feeling of appreciation for Norm's answers. The class will emulate this attitude.
  f. Never say, "Shut up!" or "Don't you know enough to keep quiet!" This antagonizes Norm and gives the appearance of teacher defeat.
  g. Suggest, in private, that he count to ten before answering, so that another pupil may have a chance to respond.

Third, there are other specific ways to encourage other voices in the class. Suggest that answers come from:
  a. Someone under eighteen (if Norm is 18 or older).
  b. Someone of the opposite sex.
  c. Someone who has a birthday this month.
  d. Someone who knows the memory verse.
  e. Someone with blue eyes (if Norm has brown).
  f. Someone in the front row.
  g. Someone who is wearing red.

Try a buzz session. Norm may dominate one small group, but he cannot speak for all the groups. Move him around, so his ability to talk will be advantageous to bashful students one week, uninterested pupils the next. If you select the reporter to share with the class, Know-it-all Norm can be selected one week, another voice the following week. He will have to be still while others report from buzz sessions.

If pupils are intimidated by Norm, avoid saying, "That's wrong!" Suggest, "That's a good idea. Does someone else have another idea?" Or, "That's the way I used to feel. Now that I've studied this verse more, I believe God is telling us ..." This attitude brings more spontaneous response from your pupils than "right-wrong" answers.

Fourth, have pupils record their reactions on a tape recorder. They will enjoy hearing their own voices, and responses can be limited to allow time for everyone. Also, try hiding the recorder and taping the class. Even Norm will see his know-it-all problem when class discussion is played back.

Fifth, ask the overzealous student to lead at discussion time. He will get to ask the questions, but he will have to secure answers from the others. He will not only get a feel for the teacher problem, but he will have to deal with both outspoken and quiet students. He will then realize his own talkativeness.

Sixth, you can help students overcome the fear of speaking aloud. Have them voice opinions on nonspiritual subjects, then lead them into opinions and applications of Scripture. Avoid laughing at opinions. Encourage quiet students with direct questions. From very bashful students, respect even a "yes" or "no" answer.

A teacher arriving early, listening to pupils talk about their likes and dislikes, gives them assurance and ease before the teacher. After class, let lingering students talk about their needs or their victories. Be available.

Seventh, most of the problem with Know-it-all Norm is a lack of teacher preparation. If the teacher plans ahead, selects appropriate ways to include others, teaches the class adequately, gives pupils places to find answers, and encourages the entire class to participate with preplanned discussion questions, results will occur.

Know-it-all Norm is not all bad. Yes, he is aggressive. He turns off some students. He is a time consumer. Maybe he has studied his lesson and wants to share his knowledge. Maybe he has been put down all week at home and needs the outlet. Maybe the teacher needs a time filler.

A slipshod lesson requires a Know-it-all Norm to fill the moments before the closing bell. An unprepared teacher may say all he knows in five minutes!

A lecturing teacher requires a Know-it-all Norm. Any interruption is better than one continuous voice from the teacher for sixty minutes. Too many teachers have the mistaken idea that if they give an hour of information, there will be an hour of learning.

An unconcerned leader requires a Know-it-all Norm. Such a student motivates the teacher to try harder. The good teacher helps straighten out Norm before the world puts him down. Love Norm and use him as a leader to draw out other students.

Know-it-all Norm is just as precious in God's sight as any other student. Tap his resources and bring him and his ways into the control of God. He will be an asset to your class.

CHAPTER FOUR
What Do You Do With Doubting Dick?

Dick looks at his teacher in disbelief. "Jesus walked on water? You must be kidding. You don't expect us to swallow that story. You know physics."

Teacher replies, "Of course, I do! That's why I believe in Jesus. He did the impossible!"

Doubting Dick slides down in his chair and the teacher realizes he has closed his mind to the lesson, but goes on. There are others to teach. After the bell, teacher holds the Bible and wonders, "What shall I do with Doubting Dick?"

Jesus did many miracles. The Bible says so, and Teacher believes the Bible! Your pupils must know Him as Creator. They must acknowledge Him as God so that power can come into their lives. Doubting Dick must recognize Jesus as God, believing in the New Testament miracles, and be willing to give his life to the Lord.

How can you translate all this to a Doubting Dick?

First, pray for guidance. The problem is bigger than a teacher's capability. Pray, "Lord, I want to reach Dick. I want You to help me with the right words. Please soften his heart in the days ahead. Give me patience and strength." Put Doubting Dick on a daily prayer list, not just a "pray when I think of it" situation. "Pray without ceasing" (1 Thessalonians 5:17).

Second, study the problem. Do some extra reading: *Mere Christianity* by C. S. Lewis and *More Than a Carpenter* by Josh McDowell. Remain firm in your own faith and let the class feel your confidence in the Bible and all its teachings.

Third, take time to know Dick better. Go to his next track meet. Cheer as he passes, and greet him with "You're quite a runner, Dick!" Maybe Doubting Dick will start to listen to one who shows such special interest.

Fourth, face the doubts in class. Maybe others have similar doubts, but are more reluctant to voice them. The following ideas will help everyone in your class.

    a. Conduct a special study of the miracles, asking why Jesus performed them.

    b. Supply paper and pencil and ask your pupils to write a 25-word reply to the statement of Doubting Dick about the miracle of Jesus walking on water.

    c. Read the papers and let pupils discuss them. Papers need not be signed. As Doubting Dick begins to like his teacher more, he may be ashamed to voice his doubts orally. A good teacher realizes this, and will not want to

turn off even the negative communication with pupils. Expressing opinions in writing will help.
  d. Assign special readings on the miracles. Discuss in class.
  e. Write a paper on difficult-to-understand Bible verses. Research in the Bible itself should convince the doubter. Make this an in-class project, if you have problems with homework assignments.
  f. Memorize 2 Timothy 3:16. Print it on the chalkboard or make an attractive bulletin board display using this Scripture.

Doubting Dick is a challenge for his teacher; he is worth your concern and extra attention. What a proud moment for you when a Doubting Dick reports a school experience where he spoke up in science class revealing his new faith! A Doubting Dick won becomes a strong resource person in the class for proving God's ability to do the impossible.

Fifth, praise the Lord for answered prayer. Do this at home, alone before the Lord, and in class before the students. Confess to your class, "When I realized some of you did not believe the Scriptures, I felt like quitting. But I prayed for you, and for myself. I especially prayed for Doubting Dick and we got to know each other better. I studied hard and prepared myself to instruct you in the wonders of God and His Word. Together we struggled over answers. Now I want to say in front of you, God has been working in our class!"

Not all Doubting Dicks will believe. Some will listen for a while then leave the class, never to return. Follow up those dropouts. Encourage them to come back and study for honest answers. If they refuse, continue to pray for them. Put literature in their hands. They may read it. Remember they are in God's care and He can break the barriers that are impossible for you.

Every community has its Doubting Dicks. They are full of doubts and enjoy their life of worldliness. Often, through love from family, years of visits and kind witnessing from Christians, Doubting Dicks may come to special programs. Then to church services occasionally. Finally, they may believe in Jesus as Savior and Lord, and want to live as a Christian. Time and patience will be the key to their obedience.

The God who walked on the water in Galilee, the God who brought life to Jonah from the belly of a great fish, the God who brought Dorcas back to life is the same God who in His own timing will change the Doubting Dicks.

Teacher, you can proclaim the truths of Scripture and believe it yourself, yet distrust God's ability to work in the lives of your students. The faith to believe what God says in His Word is the same faith that sees God at work today in the lives of your pupils.

God can transform Doubting Dick into Trusting Richard, and He can make doubting teachers into trusting instructors. The next time you look at your class and see a doubter, remember Luke 1:37, "For with God nothing shall be impossible."

CHAPTER FIVE
What Do You Do With Rebellious Rob?

Rebellious Rob is an awkward young man, with long hair straggling over his ears. His feet are enormous and clumsy on his long slender legs. Rob is in transition from child to adult. He is defiant of all adults and authority figures. He is a leader among his closest friends, and rebellious among the majority. Some members of the class abide by every word out of his mouth; others try to ignore him.

Rob waits for the teacher to look away from him and suddenly the take-home papers become a shower of tiny paper snowflakes. When he sits toward the rear, his constant conservation with buddies hinders the lesson. He coughs during prayer, hums during discussions, taps his foot during the conclusion, whistles when soft-spoken Sue answers a question, snaps his fingers when the class is reading silently.

After each class session, you are ready to pull out your hair, clobber the kid, or quit teaching. What should you do with Rebellious Rob? Pulling your hair out will only make you bald; murder will put you behind bars, and quitting will deprive the rest of the class! Look for a better way.

First, Rebellious Rob needs help. If he is allowed to continue in his present ways, he will have problems for years to come. His behavior is a cry for help. Ignore him and you will be missing an opportunity to help a young person. Why is he doing such annoying things? Probably Rebellious Rob has never learned to discipline himself. Perhaps he is lacking attention at home, and is using bad behavior to be noticed. He may be a thwarted leader. Redirected, he could become a future teacher, deacon, preacher, missionary.

Second, Rebellious Rob needs love. His actions are bringing dislike and embarrassment from teacher and class. Ask God for a special love for Rob. He is not happy the way he is. Neither are you nor your pupils. The more you dislike Rob, the worse he will act. So try to like Rob. Make a special effort to do so. Do things that show love. Greet him by name. Inquire into his weekday activities. Notice his new jacket. Congratulate him on a victory. Compliment any good behavior. If you have a genuine affection for the rebellious student, Rob will know it and react to it.

Third, Rebellious Rob is asking for understanding. At home, his parents are probably telling him what to do. At school, teachers and administrators have laid down their laws. At work, the boss demands performance. When he arrives in

Sunday-school class, the teacher is the symbol of authority. Rob rebels.

When he does mouth-off, listen to his thought pattern. Do not put him down publicly. You could suggest, "I know you have some different thoughts, Rob. Tell us about them." Or, "How would you react to this situation, Rob?" Or, "I see what you are saying, Rob. In fact, at one point in my life, I would have agreed with you!" While he is still listening, reveal a rebellion from your earlier life and how you see it now. Don't fabricate a story, but if it is true, tell it!

Fourth, Rebellious Rob needs involvement. If he likes taking the opposing view, have a debate and let him be captain of his team. Give him opportunity to answer questions, ask questions, lead a class discussion. Occupying a seat is not involvement. You need not wait until he is submissive to your teaching before using him: be ready with Scriptures and pre-planned answers against outlandish ideas.

Fifth, Rebellious Rob needs leadership. It is a necessary part of growing up to rebel against authority. Every young person goes through periods when he thinks he has the answers and that adults are stupid. Part of growing up is learning what leadership to follow. Be a good leader for Rob. Find a job he can do well. Let him excel in it and see the problems of leadership. He may change as he sees himself in other classmates.

Sixth, Rebellious Rob needs punishment. Sunday-school students come voluntarily. They can leave whenever they want to or whenever their parents want them to. How far can a teacher let a student go in disrupting a class? There has to be a limit. If Rob's rebellion continues to hinder the learning process, some sort of reprimand must take place. You will want to try one or more of the following:
  a. Ask Rob to stay after class and talk calmly to him. If you are upset, postpone the confrontation until you are calm and peaceful.
  b. Try a special look at Rob, with a pause in your teaching.
  c. Change seating arrangement. Try a semi-circle. If Rob insists on sitting in the rear of the room, try teaching from the rear.
  d. Use an assistant teacher to give Rob the attention he deserves. Team teaching is a popular method.
  e. Divide the class: those willing to listen and those who

won't listen. Assign the won't listeners to a special teacher in another room.
f. Speak to his parents, as a last resort. In most cases this is not necessary or advisable. Solve the problem with your own discipline unless there is no way to teach without outside help.
g. Apply peer pressure. Befriend some of Rob's friends and get their cooperation in helping Rob. Ask for their ideas. Suggest they talk to him about his bad manners.

Remember throughout this experience, that God loved Rob enough to send His Son to die for him. Ask God for help in reaching Rob and have faith in God's ability to win a rebellious heart.

CHAPTER SIX
What Do You Do With Silly Sarah?

During the final prayer, after a good lesson, a giggle emerges. It spreads like the measles and soon the seriousness of the hour disappears. Where did the giggle begin? Everyone knows without looking. Silly Sarah is always the one.

Silliness is an emotion that sometimes controls an individual, causing giggles at the wrong time. Young people find giggling especially unmanageable. The harder they try not to laugh, the more they do. Probably Silly Sarah has no intention of giggling during the closing prayer. She may be seriously thinking about God. But suddenly some thought or action invades her mind and she starts to titter. It grows into a laugh that arouses others in the class and soon several pupils are giggling.

Junior Highs are especially silly; some younger children may have the malady as do high schoolers and a number of adults. No one is immune. Most people, at times, find irrepressible giggles part of their makeup.

What's a teacher to do in this situation? Do you explode and keep your class late, lecturing them about the holiness of God and the importance of silence during prayers? Do you say, "If you ever do that again, I'll throw you out of class"? None of these will help. Silliness will happen again. Teacher, consider the following suggestions.

First, realize that silliness is not always controllable. Silly Sarah can learn to be serious, but she will continue to giggle, even if she does not intend to do so. A thought passing through her mind can start her, or a noise, an object, or another person.

Suppose Silly Sarah has listened to most of the lesson and is ready to pray. Does her giggle shut her off from God? Not necessarily. One Sunday Silly Sarah laughed aloud in church while the minister was preaching. She didn't intend to, but every time she looked at the old lady in front of her, the giggle started. The lady's dress was inside out. Silly Sarah did not consider how elderly the woman was, she just laughed. Her friends laughed, too. The stare of the preacher didn't help; some adults frowned, but that didn't stop the silly feeling. The giggles erupted from time to time.

Later, Silly Sarah, at home in her room, prayed, "Lord, I'm sorry. I didn't mean to laugh. Help me control myself next Sunday." This Silly Sarah was very aware of God, and that giggles were out of place in worship. But she couldn't control them!

Second, avoid anger. A teacher can be so engrossed with the lesson, and concerned that students learn it, that any disturbance cannot be tolerated. The voice becomes angry, looks unloving, threats loud and unChristian. Perhaps all the preparation and teaching are nullified by the closing lecture. Teacher knows Silly Sarah is the instigator of the giggling. How much better to:
  a. Ask Sarah to stay after class and discuss it.
  b. Let the incident pass without comment (unless it occurs often during prayer time).
  c. Suggest softly (during the prayer): "Close your lips tightly until we have completed our prayer." Or, "Get it out of your system. Everyone laugh for a minute" (during teaching session).
  d. Discuss Paul's problem in Romans 7:15-20. Apply this Scripture to the problem of Silly Sarah.
  e. Teach the meaning of prayer. Ask that eyes be closed and thoughts turned toward God. Let pupils lead the prayer, or pray in unison.

Third, have a seating plan. Sarah is silliest when she sits next to her friends. Try an alphabetical arrangement one week. No one is discriminated against. The next week put the blue eyes on one side, the brown eyes on the other. Try isolation from the group when she finds it too hard to stay serious. Do not declare, "From now on, we will sit this way!" The plan may flop; Silly Sarah may mature; or she may be just as silly no matter where she sits!

Fourth, allow time for fun. An hour of seriousness is not the best way. If something is funny, laugh with your students. Jesus had a sense of humor. He told of the ridiculous situation of a camel going through the eye of a needle. "A merry heart doeth good like a medicine" (Proverbs 17:22). Begin a class with a joke or a riddle. Build toward the quiet, respectful acceptance of the lesson.

Fifth, learn not to overreact. If a student throws a rotten egg across the room, discipline swift and strong should be forthcoming. But a giggle is not the same. It is disturbing; it can be of the devil; it can ruin a conclusion; it can have a rippling effect on the entire class. But it is not vicious (usually); it is not premeditated (usually); it is not aggressive or hateful (usually).

If a teacher throws a child out of class for being silly, what will he or she do for the rotten-egg incident? If the teacher screams at a giggling student, what shall he or she do at the tipping of chairs, tearing of workbooks, or uttering crude and rude language?

Sixth, have a plan of action. Prethink the situations that can enter the classroom. Patricia may come in late; Alexander may make funny noises during the lesson; Ruth may scribble on the table and deface it with her boyfriend's initials; Frank may hang out the window yelling at passersby. Teacher, you can think through these possible situations, and have a plan all worked out for the age level in your class.

   a. For latecomers: stay and help clean up.
   b. For funny noises: repeat them in front of the class. Avoid lectures.
   c. For defacing furniture: pupil helps refinish the furniture, and pays for any major damage done.
   d. For giggling during class: private counsel.

Often a student will act in disturbing ways just to attract attention, to avoid a boring lesson, or to be in charge. While some of your students will not want to do annoying things, it can happen when least expected. Silly Sarah is embarrassed by her actions. Public ridicule will make her feel worse. Some teachers like that: they feel their power over the group. But such tactics will not help class members. It could have the opposite effect by making the situation worse.

Seventh, look in a mirror. Remember your own shortcomings in years gone by. Remember the teenage giggle, the behavior in class and out. Develop sympathy and concern for Silly Sarah. Help her mature beyond the uncontrolled emotions of giggling into good laughter. Laugh with your class. Bend a little!

It is better to hear a student laugh than to hear a moan; better to hear a chuckle than back talk; more pleasant to hear a snicker than a smashed window.

What do you do with Silly Sarah? You endure her and love her. This is a stage of her development. Harshness can turn her from God and your class. Love and understanding will draw her to the Savior. Someday Silly Sarah will thank you for your patient concern.

CHAPTER SEVEN
What Do You Do With Daydreaming Donna?

Your pupils have their eyes fixed upon you, the teacher. The lesson progresses from the attention-getter to the important points to be made. The students are reasonably quiet, seeming to absorb the information. Are they really listening? Look at Donna.

She is well behaved and smiling, but that faraway look in her eyes should alert you that a daydreamer is present. What causes your pupil to daydream? Consider these factors:

    a. She could be bored with the class.
    b. She would rather be somewhere else.
    c. She thinks she is in love.
    d. She is tired.
    e. She finds the teacher's voice unpleasant.
    f. She is not friendly with her peers.
    g. She prefers the make-believe to the real world.

Your problem is to bring her back to reality and interest her in what's happening in the classroom. How will you accomplish this?

First, discover the daydreamer. Silly Sarah is obvious; Know-it-all Norm stands out; Doubting Dick becomes exposed as he voices an opinion. Daydreamer Donna looks like the obedient, respectful student whom any teacher can appreciate. You may think she is an ideal student. She never gets into trouble.

However, if you stop talking and start listening, you will see that Daydreamer Donna doesn't even know what you have been saying. If you have the class work on paper, you will see she doesn't move her pencil. If you ask for her opinion, she will look blankly at you. If you swish your hand in front of her eyes, she probably won't blink. If you tell everyone to change seats, she will remain in hers. Daydreamer Donna is discovered when the class proceeds from lecture to sharing.

Second, change the teaching method. It is easy to daydream during a talk or lecture. One-way communication lends itself to wandering minds. And wandering minds are the first step into daydreaming. A teacher who stands up front and reads a lesson, lectures a message, or declares a sermon to a class will lose more than one daydreamer pupil.

As you work to bring Donna into the reality of your teaching, you must use a method that requires special attention.

Such methods include:
   a. Flash cards
   b. Puzzles
   c. Overhead projector
   d. Tape recorders
   e. Filmstrips
   f. Unended stories
   g. Buzz sessions (small group discussions)
   h. Outlines
   i. Quizzes
   j. Direct questioning
   k. Dramatization
   l. Circle responses
   m. Written opinions

The method must involve the pupil. Only then will Daydreamer Donna's mind be forced to stay with the curriculum. Remember: overuse of any good method can also become an escape to daydreams.

Third, acquaint yourself with the student's background. If your method of teaching is already varied and exciting, perhaps the student has another problem. Help her if you can. Daydreamer Donna will miss much of life if she continues in her way. Compile information about Donna.
   a. Have all pupils fill out a questionnaire. Ask for name, address, age, education, hobbies, family members.
   b. Inquire from the minister if he knows the family. Such information is confidential.
   c. Acquire previous record from former teachers. Information cards should be passed along in Sunday school.
   d. Visit in the home. Make an appointment and keep it. Stay a limited time. Show an interest in the family.
   e. Arrive early in class and be ready to inquire into Donna's activities. Show interest in her accomplishments.
   f. Invite her to your home for a meal, asking another student to come also.
   g. Get to know her at class parties. Social activities reveal new aspects of pupil personality.
   h. Use the telephone. Call Donna and see how she is doing on a particular assignment or a problem.

Fourth, praise the student for progress. If you do not notice the pupil's improved attitude, she will slip back into her old ways. Of course, the teacher has a class full of individuals.

You cannot concentrate unduly on just one pupil. Yet, how long does it take to say, "You're doing well!"? Here are ways to praise and ways not to:

Ways to praise

    a. After class, remark to Donna: "It was a joy to have you in class today!"
    b. Declare, "I like Donna's comment. Can you add to it?"
    c. Write her a card saying, "Donna your remark on prayer was so helpful."
    d. Before class, greet Donna with these words, "Donna, I appreciated your interest last week. Would you mind heading a buzz group today?"

Ways not to praise

    a. "Did you all notice how attentive Donna was today?"
    b. "What do you know, class. Donna isn't daydreaming today."
    c. "Why haven't you opened your mouth this morning, Donna?"
    d. "Well, at least you're alive and kicking!"
    e. "Not bad for someone from another planet!"
    f. "Come out of your daydream and be a part of us again!"

An unnoticed student will learn little. A praised individual will reach for higher goals. Try it! Both the student and the teacher will like it.

Philosopher George Santayana said, "The dreamer can know no truth, not even about his dream, except by waking out of it." The duty of each instructor is to guide the Daydreamer Donnas to wake up, to love life, and to live it in Jesus Christ. To lead Donna back from her dream world, be an exciting teacher with a well-prepared lesson taught in a fascinating way that will make it impossible for any student to ignore.

CHAPTER EIGHT
What Do You Do With Troubled Tom?

When a sorrowing young man like Troubled Tom enters your classroom you have an awesome responsibility. You must help him to overcome his trouble, or encourage him to exist in his anxiety and have victory over it. If you truly knew the hearts of your students, you would discover several with hidden pain and grief. The troubles of the world come down heavy on young people. They may not have the comfort of a close walk with God. They need spiritual guidance.

Problems of family, school, and work may be the immediate cause of their trouble. Some can handle their lives; others are weighed down with the burdens. In both cases, you must try to be a help and a stabilizing influence.

Probably Troubled Tom will not open up and declare his problem. You will have to discover it yourself, and consider ways to help him.

First, to help Troubled Tom you must find him. If you rush into class, have a hurried conclusion to your lesson, then dash off to the next service without interaction, you will not find the troubled pupil. Knowing and caring about Tom is the gospel in action. In him you may find a part of Rebellious Rob or Sinful Sam. Many characteristics will focus in on Troubled Tom. How can a busy teacher with a dozen other students discover and help the troubled one? Especially if his aim is to keep the knowledge secret? There are ways.

    a. Look for Troubled Tom through discussions. He may drop hints in his answers.

    b. Look for Troubled Tom through questionnaires. If he has a one-parent home, he may be hurting,

    c. Look for Troubled Tom through outside activities. Problems may lead him to skip social events.

    d. Look for Troubled Tom through specific prayer. Have class members write down their biggest needs, their strongest temptations.

    e. Look for Troubled Tom with your eyes. His sad or disturbed expression and his behavior are revealing.

Second, to help Troubled Tom is to meet his need. Many people prefer to bypass problems, or pretend they don't exist. The issues must be faced. They will not go away.

Tom may be troubled because of a divorce in the family. Class lessons can point out the sufficiency of Christ in broken homes without singling out Tom. Chances are, more than one pupil may be coping with divorce, either at home or with a friend or relative. Tom may be troubled because of money problems. His parents may argue about money. They may not have enough to pay bills; food may be scarce; college out of the question. Or the making of money may be so important that the family is neglected. Tom finds himself in the middle of the squeeze.

Tom may be troubled by sickness. Perhaps he has diabetes or a heart problem. Maybe his father has cancer, or his grandmother could be dying. Any of these situations are hard for Tom to handle. When you know the problem, stress the healing power of God. Pray in class for the illness, unless Tom wishes to keep his trouble private. Let him know you are praying for him. Talk about death and the home in Heaven. Most lessons can lend themselves to specific problems.

Read comforting Bible verses. "If ye abide in me, and my words abide in you, ye shall ask what ye will, and it shall be done unto you" (John 15:7). "And this is the confidence that we have in him, that, if we ask any thing according to his will, he heareth us" (1 John 5:14).

If Troubled Tom cannot find help in his Bible class, where will he find it? Never go around a problem. Deal with it.

Third, to help Troubled Tom is to be alone with him. Privacy is important for some discussions. People in stress do not like to open up in front of a group. They will suffer inside and alone. If you know Tom has a problem, take him out for a sandwich in a quiet place where you can talk and share ideas. Look for a specific area where you or the class can help. Does Tom need transportation? Does he want a good listener? Should he have pastoral counseling?

Sometimes it is easier to spout our faith to a group than it is on a one-to-one basis. Troubled Tom needs your time and your personal attention. If he is alone in church, sit with him; if he heads for home alone after service, catch up to him and drive him home.

Fourth, to help Troubled Tom is to follow through. When you have convinced Tom that you can and will help him, be available when he calls. Late some night he may telephone you saying, "My Dad's drunk. Can I come over for a while?" If you are tired or busy, he will think you didn't mean it when you said, "Let me know if I can help."

If he calls and you are genuinely busy, take a moment on the phone and pray with him or talk to him, suggesting a comforting verse of Scripture. Make an appointment to get back to him. "I'm in a meeting right now, Tom, but if you can be over in an hour, I'd be glad to visit with you." A troubled person will creep deeper into his sorrow if put off indefinitely. Teacher, you may not be involved often with such problems, but when you find a Troubled Tom, make yourself available.

Fifth, to help Troubled Tom teach him that this life will have problems until Jesus comes again. The Christian life does not promise all laughter and no tears. Jesus said, "In the world ye shall have tribulation: but be of good cheer; I have overcome the world" (John 16:33). The psalmist wrote, "But the salvation of the righteous is of the Lord: he is their strength in the time of trouble" (Psalm 37:39).

Pupils in your class may think coming into Jesus will make life perfect. He does make it complete and filled with joy, but that will come about in the midst of troubles and trials as well as when everything is going right. You must be honest with your students and let them know the reality, then they will not be overwhelmed by troubles. They can face bravely their trials with a peace that only Jesus can give.

Sixth, to help Troubled Tom is to guide him to praise God even in times of trouble. The early Christians praised God together on many occasions. Lead Troubled Tom to praise the Lord for victory in his situation. He will be grateful for your teaching as he experiences life's difficulties in the future, as well as the present.

Every Sunday-school class has its Troubled Tom. God has placed him there for you to help. God has placed you there to be a counselor. Face the calamity. Solve it with God's help. Tom may be ready at this time to accept Christ or to dedicate his life to service. Use the circumstance for God's glory.

Teacher, be sensitive to your students' needs. Help Troubled Tom!

CHAPTER NINE
What Do You Do With Friendless Fran?

Fran has no friends. She arrives at class alone, and sits by herself. The rest of the students either do not notice or do not care that she is lonely.

Sometimes the situation is worse in a Christian group than in other circumstances. Christians feel very close to each other, and form a bond that is precious. A newcomer may find it hard to enter that exclusive company.

Christians may not realize what they are doing. Perhaps they find the oneness in Christ so tremendous that they live in a closed little world. Perhaps they resent anyone who would make a change in the status quo. Such exclusiveness turns away outsiders, and denies them the opportunity to hear the gospel and become a part of that oneness.

How can you help Friendless Fran?

First, notice Friendless Fran. An observant teacher takes note of the popular students, the outgoing, and the shy people. From your vantage point, you can be an influence for integration of various personalities. Your job involves more than passing facts from your brain or quarterly to other heads. Your teaching mission includes reaching and teaching the whole person. Friendless Fran will be obvious if you open your eyes and really see. One Sunday without friends in your class is enough!

Second, make friends personally with Friendless Fran. Your friendliness will influence others. Here are ways for you to be friendly with a pupil:

   a. Know her name. Never have to say, "Who are you?"
   b. Invite her to sit with you during church service.
   c. Visit in her home.
   d. Call her on the phone when she is absent.
   e. Compliment her on her attire, or hairstyle.
   f. Remember her birthday with a card.
   g. Give her a responsibility in the class.
   h. Take time to listen to her.

If Friendless Fran is genuinely liked by her teacher and she knows it, she will have confidence to try other friendships.

Third, understand the problems some have in making friends. Because Friendless Fran feels rejected by others, she shuts herself off from further entanglements with people. Her reasons may include:

   a. Sensitive about appearance. If Friendless Fran is plain looking, awkward, has skin blemishes, or a physical

problem, she feels others shun her. If Fran has a speech problem or wears odd clothing, or in any other way does not fit the mold of her peers, she may be left in the cold.
  b. Hurt by a precious association. When the teacher discovers this reason for Fran's attitude, you can point out how most friendships do not end that way. Everyone has some troublesome relationships. Forget those and launch into new friendships. Tell Fran to make new acquaintances. Some will blossom into true friends.
  c. Afraid to speak. It may be painful for Fran to talk. This leads others to believe she is unfriendly. In familiar surroundings at home, she may let down the barriers, but in public she is reluctant to speak. Tell her she has much to offer. She should pray for God's help in conversation whenever the opportunity arises.
  d. Feels disliked by peers. Tell her to give people a chance to know her. Instruct the class to welcome Fran into their circle. Have someone greet her and assigned to sit with her. Keep working with her and class members until friendly relationships emerge.

Fourth, awaken the class to its mission. Every class ought to grow. Challenge your pupils to welcome new people. Encourage pupils to become known as the "friendly" class.
  a. Vote on a class name that includes "Friends" or "Friendly" in it.
  b. Include "reach out" as part of the Bible instruction. Use Luke 14:23; 2 Corinthians 5:20; Mark 16:15; Ephesians 4:32.
  c. Be specific about shunning newcomers. Explain that Jesus loves everyone. He reached beyond His circle of twelve apostles to include others.
  d. Appoint special greeters, who welcome and introduce people who come to your class.
  e. If Friendless Fran is still left out, meet with class officers and discuss ways to show love and concern for Fran.

Fifth, be an example of friendliness. If the teacher shuns certain people in the church, you can expect no better from your class. If you are too busy to seek new friends, you cannot expect your students to take the time. Friendship is taught in Scripture. "A man that hath friends must show himself friendly: and there is a friend that sticketh closer than a brother" (Proverbs 18:24). Such comradeship ought to exist in the Sunday-school class. The teacher can lead the way.

Sixth, share the friendliness of the class with others. At a teachers' meeting mention the efforts of your class to be friendly. Stress the importance of this. Let others know your good feelings toward students. Tell Susan's parents how much you appreciate Susan's willingness to be a friend to Fran and how it brought Fran out of her loneliness.

All of us need to meet new people and make them part of our circle of acquaintances. Watch for the Friendless Fran in your class. Bring her closer to Jesus that she may know the greatest Friend of all. "Ye are my friends, if ye do whatsoever I command you" (John 15:14).

CHAPTER TEN
What Do You Do With Sinful Sam?

Sinful Sam? Not in Sunday school? Never in Bible study? Praise the Lord, sinners do come sometimes! If Sinful Sam is in your class, accept the challenge. He needs a Savior and the life-changing message of the gospel.

The Bible says, "For all have sinned, and come short of the glory of God" (Romans 3:23). Also, "There is none righteous, no, not one" (v. 10). Every pupil has weaknesses and needs the nurture of other Christians. Most people, however, try to live within the law; they are not blatant wrongdoers. Yet, they need the Lord just as much as Sinful Sam does. The difference is that Sinful Sam is proud of his misdeeds and brags about them openly. What will you do with Sam?

First, recognize Sinful Sam's condition. Usually you say of your students, "They are not so bad." You close your eyes to obvious problems. "No one in my class would do such a thing!" Even if he brags about his deeds, you consider them an exaggeration. You must see Sinful Sam as he is, to be able to help him. Be aware of the talk and activities of class members. Notice their hangouts, their friends, their interests, their ability at school or work, their dress, and their attitude toward authority. Sinful Sam may spend a lot of time with the wrong crowd. Remember that some people are all talk. That will have to be discerned for each pupil. But if the actions equal the claims, Sinful Sam needs your help.

Second, learn to love Sinful Sam, even though you hate his sin. How easy to say, "I love everybody." How tough to fulfill this ideal. There are some individuals who are repulsive. Sinful Sam may have a bad influence over other class members. You may wish he'd stay away. Sinful Sam needs to feel genuine love or he will leave, maybe to be lost forever. Christian love is more than human love: it is guided by God who loved Sinful Sam enough to send His Son to die for him. From God's perspective, Sam is a great possibility. Love comes through prayer and study of the Word. Keep praying and searching the Word until you can say in your heart, "I do love Sinful Sam!" Your disposition will change toward him, and he will be reached easier because God's love will flow through you to him.

Third, do not be afraid to teach against sin. Too often teachers are scared to talk against the sins of those present in the classroom: to condemn cheating if a cheater is there; to denounce divorce if that is troubling a family in your class; to discuss marijuana if a pot smoker is in the room. The challenge is to discuss specific sins with concern and love for the individual, not hate or bitterness. Don't point a finger at Sinful Sam, for others have sins, too. At every opportunity stress God's forgiveness of sins. Sinful Sam must become aware of God's displeasure with sin. Only then can he understand and pray for pardon through Christ. Be a daring teacher, unafraid to teach what God says about sin and forgiveness.

Fourth, arrange for a one-to-one encounter with Sinful Sam. Don't let him think he is being singled out, for you should try to spend time with every student. An informal meeting is better than a structured situation. A coffee shop has a nonthreatening atmosphere, or your own dining-room table. A walk through a quiet park, or even a talk in the back pew after church could be used. Such a session should include:
    a. Be a listener. Too many talks are one-sided: all teacher.
    b. Have a Bible handy. Let answers come from God's Word.
    c. Let Sam read the Word for himself.
    d. Have prayer with him. Even if he is nervous, he'll appreciate it. Don't force him to pray until he is ready.

Fifth, guide the class to follow Christ not worldly people. Many young people are attracted by the glamour of sin. If Sam has money jingling in his pockets, or influential friends, his classmates may be tempted to go his way. The class has to be taught that God's way is the only way. Although Sinful Sam is important, and it is the responsibility of the teacher to win him to Jesus, it cannot be at the sacrifice of the entire class.

Sometimes, when teacher gives attention to a needy individual, you seem to be saying to the others, "I'd spend more time with you if you had a serious problem." Help all your pupils with wholesome recreation and one-to-one conferences. Each individual is important. Guide each pupil in Christian growth. Everyone should face the responsibility to make a commitment to Christ.

Sixth, teach Sinful Sam about God's love and God's judgment. Most Bible lessons can be adapted to proclaim the love of God. Whether it is the creation story or the Beatitudes, whether it be Amos or Peter, the message is there: God loves you and cares for you. He wants to deliver you from His judgment. If Sinful Sam comes to Jesus, he may have a hard time leaving the old ways and walking God's way. Be there, ready to help him through the difficulties.

Sinful Sam may come and go. You may not see him make a decision. But be sure he hears the gospel while in your class, then when you get to Heaven, you may discover he is there to greet you. Because you taught him and showed him hope in the Bible, he may eventually turn to the Lord.

Some teachers wish Sinful Sam would stay away. They are afraid to face him. But he needs to know. Be thankful for his presence; with prayer and concern seek to lead him to God. Remember, "For with God nothing shall be impossible" (Luke 1:37).

CHAPTER ELEVEN
What Do You Do With Unloved Larry?

To be unloved is a sad situation. Do you have an Unloved Larry in your class? Would you recognize him if he were among your pupils? Unloved Larry may be ridiculed, shunned, shutout of activities because for some reason he seems unlovable. Will you care enough to discover *why* he is unloved? Will you find ways to help him? He does not need your pity, but he does need your understanding and love.

Some people are unloved because of their mentality. A pupil with a low IQ or poor coordination may be unwelcome in some Sunday-school classes. Some are unloved because of physical deformities: struggling to walk, straining to hear, faltering from blindness. They are an embarrassment to others who avoid them, making fun of them, rarely pausing to love them. Yet Jesus was concerned with unlovely people. His love for the crippled, the blind, the sick is an example for all. You and your students must open your arms to those who struggle with physical problems.

The unloved person may be lacking in human love, but God loves everyone. And He loves the unlovable. In the church there should be no Unloved Larry. How can you help show love if an Unloved Larry appears in your class?

First, seek out Unloved Larry and be a friend to him. An observant teacher will notice Larry in the class, but you must also look beyond the classroom door. Larry may be in a church service, too afraid to enter a small class. Larry may be outside the church, hesitating by the entrance. Bring him in and show him the love of Jesus and the concern of His followers. You may see Larry in your neighborhood and bring him to the church where he can find genuine love. Unloved Larry will never come to you and declare, "No one loves me, will you?" You must reach out to him.

Second, help Unloved Larry become more confident. Ask other pupils to aid him. Be patient if his speech is slow. Listen carefully, give him confidence. Let him write his class answers. Assign one person to interpret for him. If he needs therapy, help arrange for it. If personal hygiene is his difficulty, arrange for help from the local health board, or a loving older Christian.

Third, help Unloved Larry make friends. This will involve study and time: finding a willing Christian in your class and teaching him how to love Larry. Actually, love for Larry is the gospel in action. If Larry can see God's love in practice, he can more easily comprehend the love of God. If Larry is left unloved, he will drift from the church, perhaps never to come to Christ at all. 1 Corinthians 13 has the pattern: "Love is kind ... beareth all things ... endureth all things."

Be sure Unloved Larry is invited to parties, outside activities, and fellowship opportunities. Let Larry's new friends get involved in finding transportation, helping with needs he may have, and taking time to be available for talking, shopping, eating out, or whatever interests he may have. Possibly one afternoon a week could be special for Larry. You may find it not only a service, but a pleasure, to help this pupil.

Fourth, teach Unloved Larry about God's love. This can be done in several ways:
   a. Express God's love through the weekly lessons.
   b. Give Larry and other pupils a tract about love. Mail one to Larry, with a personal note.
   c. Put your arm across Larry's shoulder and say, "God loves you, Larry, and so do we!"
   d. Ask the class to do a special study on various subjects. Have one group study God's love. Include Larry in that group.
   e. Select some love Scriptures for Larry to memorize.

Fifth, turn Larry's thoughts to others who also have needs. Help him find a way to serve. Most likely Unloved Larry's eyes are drawn inward; he thinks he has the worst problems in all the world. Allow him to discover people with serious defects, and let him see how he can help them. Larry could accomplish this through:
   a. Assist in a nursing home ministry.
   b. Help an assistant Sunday-school teacher.
   c. Write letters to lonely people.
   d. Participate in hospital visitation.
   e. Assist in conducting Bible studies at a half-way house.

These suggestions would take training and extra helps. Larry would suffer if he failed in his ministry. Back him up with instruction, counseling, personal encouragement, adequate help, and with prayer. Challenge him, but don't assign him more than he can successfully handle.

People develop as they serve. They forget themselves when they become involved with other people. Larry is no different. He can do much to help others who may feel unloved. Pupils with problems need help, and the best way to help them may be to see their potential in learning to help others. Do not deprive them of the joy of serving!

Love forms a chain reaction. You receive love from God. You pass it along to Unloved Larry. He accepts that love and goes on to share it with others. Unloved Larry becomes a loving servant of a loving Lord.

CHAPTER TWELVE
What Do You Do With Slow-learner Sally?

Slow-learner Sally is coming to your Sunday-school class. Other teachers have mentioned her to you and you want to be ready for her. What makes Sally a slow learner? Is she from an unstable home, where divorce, death, or disunity cause problems? Is Sally slow because of lack of interest by her parents? Maybe she never learned the joy of books, the thrill of discovering new things or desiring achievement.

Maybe she is a slow learner because of physical problems: sight, mobility, hearing, extended sickness. Maybe her IQ is low. Whatever the cause, Slow-learner Sally is in your Sunday-school class and needs your love. What will you do to help this special pupil?

First, have good communication with the parents. A parent should feel free to talk to the teacher. "My daughter has problems with reading. She is a happy, loving child. Just don't ask her to read aloud." This helps you, the teacher to use caution in involving Sally in a reading activity. Sometimes, parents are embarrassed to tell of their child's shortcomings. They keep it a secret. This hurts the child and hinders instruction, but respect their feelings. Be positive with parents about Sally's abilities. Learn what to expect of Slow-learner Sally from her previous teachers, but allow for change and development in your class.

Second, study into the learning disability. Go to a public school and ask for an interview with a schoolteacher. Seek his or her advice on books to read, students to observe, and a plan of action. Introduce yourself as a Sunday-school teacher interested in helping Slow-learner Sally. Most teachers will be happy to share their knowledge about slow learners. They realize slow learners are often neglected outside the schoolroom. Ask to sit in a class that has integrated slow learners with other students. Take note of the way the child participates, her opportunities to excel, her frustration, her friendships, and special needs. Also observe the reactions of other students.

Write down specific questions to ask after class. Take notes on methods the teacher uses to involve slow learners and the words of encouragement, and observe the way he or she lets the children solve situations themselves. This will guide you in your own approach to teaching Slow-learner Sally.

Third, accept Slow-learner Sally for who she is. She will not change from her low mental capacity to a genius in your class. Don't expect it. Help her to do her best. Each time she fails, she will think less of herself, so don't push too hard. Even if you were able to give 100% of your time to teaching and working with Sally, she would not become an Einstein. She probably would take intensive instruction as a threat from an unloving teacher. Slow-learner Sally is unable to grasp truths at a rapid pace. Yet she may be able to learn at a steady rate. The teacher must realize the capabilities and love her for it.

What if it does take Sally two weeks to learn John 3:16 while the others pick it up in ten minutes? Perhaps Sally will remember it long after the others forget. And if Sally learns the meaning of the verse, even if she never memorizes it, the task of teaching is accomplished.

Fourth, guide the other students to love and care for Slow-learner Sally. Some children are left out of activities because they are different: skin a different color, hair straggly, an arm paralyzed, eyes crossed, or a slow mind. Lead your pupils to be sympathetic and understanding. They may cry when someone is hurt; they will help someone who falls; they will encourage someone who is behind in a game. Develop that tender characteristic. Find ways to encourage love and care for Slow-learner Sally:

    a. Teach pupils to be patient with her.
    b. Choose one or two students who are leaders and assign them specific ways to help Sally.
    c. Discipline anyone who takes pleasure in tormenting Sally.
    d. Let Sally be captain of a team occasionally.
    e. Arrange seating so she is away from antagonizers.
    f. Compliment those who show love and concern.

Fifth, allow Slow-learner Sally to participate in activities where she can outperform the others. Sally finds it difficult to do some of the basic skills that come naturally to average learners. But she may have talent in drawing. Let her make the visuals and be sure the class knows she did it. If her expertise is friendliness, let her call others to remind them of activities. If her talent is setting up the classroom or decorating the bulletin board, let her be in charge. Let her bake a cake for a birthday. Perhaps she can sing well. Let her open the class with a solo. Discover her abilities in some of these ways:

a. Home contact. It is imperative that you have close contact with the parents.
b. Build up Sally's confidence in you. Help her feel free to converse with you.
c. Make her feel important to the class. Let her "read" a verse she has memorized.
d. Find an occasion to let her display her hobby and talk about it. If she collects coins, make use of her collection with some Bible story.
e. Help her prepare to tell an experience that would interest the class. Other students may share also.

Sixth, the most important step in aiding Slow-learner Sally is to lead her to Jesus Christ. During life she may be ridiculed and excluded, but help her find strength in knowing God. She can be taught that God has said, "I will never leave thee, nor forsake thee" (Hebrews 13:5).

God loves Sally as He loves the professor or the astronaut. Today's generation has put so much stress on a high IQ, a college education, and high achievement, that Slow-learner Sally may be overlooked.

Pray for Sally, take time to present the simple truths of the gospel and give opportunity for her to receive the Lord into her life. Teacher, help her to grow as a Christian. She may astound the entire class in her faith and trust in the Savior.

CHAPTER THIRTEEN
What Do You Do With Domineering Dominick?

Domineering Dominick can take over your class. He has the ability to overrule the teacher and force minds to listen to him. He has discovered that he can manipulate others and enjoys doing this in your classroom. Domineering means ruling over, bossing, being a dictator. Dominick must have a keen mind; he knows how to influence people; he is obnoxious!

You could send him home with this warning: "Don't come back until you are willing to let ME teach!" Or, you could shout, "Shut up!" Or, you could just endure him. But there are better ways to deal with Dominick. He is in your class to be ministered to and to be taught. Therefore, you must discover what you can do to help him.

First, learn what makes him tick. Dominick has an analytical mind, and he uses psychology, even though he does not know the subject through classroom study. Because he has learned that certain tactics cause people to react in particular patterns, he uses this to his own advantage. Dominick has a need to be in charge of the situation. He feels unloved or insignificant, and thrills at the opportunity to use his words to change the conversation, or in some other way bring himself into focus.

Probably he has verbal skills above those of his peers and thrives on leadership. Being in charge helps him twist people to agree with his philosophy.

Second, let it be known who is boss in the class. Dominick may know more than the teacher in a certain subject, he may be able to argue a point more persuasively, he may be blessed with a louder voice, but he must learn he is not in charge. You, the teacher, must always be in control of the activities and the instructions, unless you relieve yourself of that role for a temporary time during class.

To prove to the students who the leader is, try one or more of the following:
   a. Insist on order before beginning a class session.
   b. Declare the procedure for discussion. Allow time for students to speak, with a final word by teacher.
   c. Talk beyond the allotted time will not be tolerated. If Dominick carries on beyond the time, he can be dismissed, kept after class, forbidden to participate next time, or brought before an authority figure.
   d. Eliminate discussion until he is ready to cooperate. Substitute a film, buzz groups, written answers.

e. Make friends with Domineering Dominick and point out his disturbance in class. He may think you need his wisdom and that you like his behavior.

Third, find ways to use his sharp abilities. How beneficial for all to have an expert persuader in class, if he were presenting the message of the lesson. How tremendous to have Dominick debating for the Lord instead of disrupting the class. Learn to use Dominick in positive ways.

a. Have a debate on creation and evolution. Meet with Dominick and ask him to defend the creation by God. Give him guidance. He will suddenly be important, and his skills will be put to good use. His mind will comprehend the arguments, and his powers of influence will lead others to agree with the Scriptures.

b. Let Dominick lead a buzz group. He may dominate three other students, but it will be for only five minutes, and the rest of the class will be able to speak up in separate groups.

c. Have students present reports. Dominick will do well. To keep others from being reluctant to follow him, have his report last.

d. Ask Dominick to teach the class some Sunday. Help him prepare. Warn him about not letting one student monopolize the class. He will see the problem from the teacher's viewpoint.

e. Direct his talent for leadership. Help him learn to use his gifts for God.

Fourth, do not allow the enthusiasm of Domineering Dominick to be squelched. He has to learn to cooperate; he must submit to some authority; he must learn to be polite. How aggravating he can be! Teachers dislike him and want to move him out of their class, but that accomplishes nothing for him.

What an opportunity for a teacher to be the instrument of God to lead Domineering Dominick to use his talents in service for God! What a great preacher he could be! What an avid soul winner he could become! God can transform lives, even domineering personalities.

God made Dominick for a purpose. Satan may be in control for a while, but with instruction and discipline, Dominick may become a great Christian leader. You should look at each student, thinking what God can do with that life. In the developing stages of Christian growth, few people have the necessary submissive attitudes.

Domineering Dominick will try your patience and almost lead you to quit teaching, but labor on, seeking the prayers of friends who will understand and not gossip. Shed a few tears, if necessary, but love and guide him while he is in your class. Someday he will remember your love and patience, saying, "That was when I began to grow up!"

CHAPTER FOURTEEN
What Do You Do With Resentful Roger?

Resentful Roger is in Sunday school nearly every Sunday. Not because he wants to learn—he has to attend to be eligible to play on the softball team. He resents spending Sunday morning in a classroom. He is under authority at school all week; his parents are always bugging him at home. He is irritated with in-charge people. Except for his love of sports, he would rather sleep until noon.

Even when you expect pupils to be quiet in class, he thinks the whole world is against him. When you ask the students to open their Bibles, he resents it because someone is telling him what to do.

The German philosopher, Friedrich Nietzsche said, "Nothing on earth consumes a man more quickly than the passion of resentment." If resentment is allowed to blossom into the mind and heart, it will fill the entire person with bitterness.

Is it possible to guide Roger from his resentment on to a productive life-style? What should you do?

First, determine not to grow weary. His refusal to obey and bored disinterest are meant to frustrate you and test your endurance. You will need the grace of God to continue loving Resentful Roger while he shakes his head in disgust. You will need a sweet Christian disposition to bear his moans during classtime. Roger will try you to the point of giving up. But God is stronger. His love is more enduring and His power to change lives is more thorough than one bitter young person. Keep in touch with God through prayer for both Roger and yourself. You may think Resentful Roger is not perceiving any of the lessons in the weekly classes. Yet, the Holy Spirit can penetrate a closed mind, and something you say may be just the words to break the barriers. Keep on teaching your lessons as planned and trust the results to God.

Second, show sincere interest in Resentful Roger.
 a. Greet him as he arrives in class. At first he may not respond, or he may just grunt. Secretly, he will be pleased you noticed him.
 b. Attend his softball games when possible. Cheer for him. Compliment his achievements.
 c. Invite Resentful Roger to your home some evening. He may not come, but invite him.
 d. Plan a party and be sure Roger can attend.

Do not avoid problem pupils. They need your time and concern. Resentment should not cause you to walk separate paths. Jesus had patience with those who resented Him.

Third, guide Resentful Roger into a special friendship in the class. What Roger won't take from you, he may take from a friend. You and Roger's friend could have a common goal: to reach Roger for Christ. Pray with Roger's friend and help him see he has a mission field right in his Bible class. Both pupils will benefit in this sharing process.

Fourth, use subtle discipline. Resentful Roger is asking for a firm hand. Give it to him. Otherwise, he will feel he is succeeding and will try all the harder. No Sunday-school teacher or Christian worker can use physical punishment. A spank, a tap on the hand, a slap across the lips—avoid, no matter how strong the provocation to do so. Try some of the following ways to discipline Resentful Roger:

a. Have another adult sit in the class, possibly the coach of the softball team. If the coach is also a Bible teacher, ask him to co-teach with you.
b. Ask Roger to sit by himself until he is willing to participate.
c. Since he is acting juvenile, send him to a younger class in the Sunday school, after clearing with that teacher.
d. As a last resort, put him out of the classroom. If it means no more ball games for him, he may try harder to please.
e. Let Resentful Roger know what you expect of him in your class; be firm and friendly.

Most Resentful Rogers will outgrow their distaste for authority. Time is a healer of this disease. Sometimes, however, a personality is so forged during a resentful period that the attitude becomes a lifelong characteristic. As a Bible teacher you must pray and work with great diligence until you see progress in the life of Resentful Roger. God loves him; it is the actions that displease Him. Remember Roger is a sinner in need of a Savior. If he learns to love Jesus, he will want to change. Help Roger discipline his life!

CHAPTER FIFTEEN
What Do You Do With Super-spiritual Sharon?

Sharon is the hope of every teacher. She is super sweet and always smiling. She is regular in attendance, carries her Bible, and talks freely about Jesus. Yet, other class members turn away from Super-spiritual Sharon. Why is she disliked by her peers?

Sharon always answers questions the right way. She reports that she prays every day, studies her Bible for hours, and always has a witnessing experience to describe. You would like to believe Sharon. You want every young person to spend time reading the Bible and praying. You would be thrilled if every student would tell others about Jesus. Pupils like Sharon make your teaching worthwhile.

Careful analysis, however, may portray more than a dedicated Christian girl; it may reveal exaggeration to impress the teacher. Or, Super-spiritual Sharon may hope to gain recognition among her classmates and win the praise of people. There is a language Christians learn that puts believers in good standing with others of the faith. Sharon has learned the expressions that give her a spiritual halo.

So, what should you do with Super-spiritual Sharon? Why would you want to change a "spiritual" student? She may be sincere.

First, determine how sincere Super-spiritual Sharon is. This will require great tact, as well as observation. Get to know her better, her activities and interests. How much time does she spend on school activities, piano lessons, homework, helping with household duties? Simple arithmetic of the hours in the week will reveal whether she has exaggerated about her time for spiritual things.

Second, discover why she overstated her Christian activities. Sharon probably does know Jesus in a real way. She has come to accept Him into her life and is trying to live the Christian life. She knows she should be doing certain things to please the Lord. Sharon even finds pleasure declaring in class that she and her parents always get along. They agree on all regulations! Her peers think that is impossible. Does Super-spiritual Sharon believe that statement will please the teacher? Why does she boast about her accomplishments? Why stretch the truth? Examine these reasons:

    a. She hears you tell the class to improve their Bible reading, prayer life, witnessing, and family relationships. She wants to please you.

b. She strives for perfection.
   c. She wants the preacher to recognize her as a special Christian.
   d. She feels left out by her peers and wants someone to notice her.
   e. She never sees your shortcomings. She thinks her teacher is perfect.
   f. She is at the top academically; she wants to do the same spiritually.
   g. She once exaggerated her spiritual life and made a big hit. Now she doesn't know how to get back on the level.

Third, help Super-spiritual Sharon see (or hear) herself. Some people make false statements not even realizing what they are doing. Sharon may be in such a predicament. She may think that if she desires to study the Bible for hours, it is as good as doing it. Her problem must be dealt with, because God cannot tolerate lies, false pride, or hypocrisy. Consider these ways to help Super-spiritual Sharon:
   a. Begin praying for an opening in class to discuss hypocrisy. Do not mention names or embarrass anyone.
   b. Plan private sessions with Sharon until she outgrows the problem.
   c. Admit areas where you are struggling in your own life. Avoid any appearance of perfection.
   d. Congratulate the achievements; be compassionate with the failures among your students.
   e. Help Sharon to admit that she has overstated some of her good deeds. Others in the class may be exaggerating their wrongdoing. Both attitudes need adjustment.
   f. Make a recording of class sessions. If Sharon has boasted, she will hear herself on the playback.

When Super-spiritual Sharon can tell her friends, "I didn't really pray that long, I just thought it was a long time," she will then be on her way to spiritual maturity.

Fourth, teach Super-spiritual Sharon God's forgiveness. Do not show her the mistakes in her life and leave her to wallow in guilt. Often an action is condemned with no help in solving it. The ideas above will help, but the ultimate help is from God. Sharon must be assured that "God loves you and forgives you. Just tell God that you've stretched the truth and you are sorry." Pray with her, love her, admire her for her willingness to see her sin of hypocrisy and change. Share the following verses with all your students, as well as Sharon. The verses deal with forgiveness of sin.

1 John 1:9	Psalm 32:5
Isaiah 1:18	Psalm 106:6
2 Samuel 24:10	Psalm 51:2
Proverbs 28:13	Psalm 38:18

Fifth, use Super-spiritual Sharon to help others. Sharon is not alone in her sin. Many people give glowing accounts of spiritual experiences. Some invent gross sins to make their conversion experience more exciting. Every student must learn that false proclamations hinder the work of the gospel, turn others away, and lead to further sin.

Sharon can share with the class, when she is ready, that her tongue was telling more than what was actually true in her life. If she can admit her exaggeration, her peers will respect her and take her into their circle.

Past experiences are not wasted. No one should commit sin just to overcome it and let it be of service. However, sin may overtake people and keep them from the Lord forever. If sin is in a life, if it is discovered, confessed and forgiven, then that individual should thank the Lord and share with others.

Super-spiritual Sharon can become a humble, growing Sharon!

HIDDEN TRUTH REVEALED SERIES

ADAM
Had to DIE

HERBERT J. BRUNSWICK, JR.

xulon PRESS

Copyright © 2014 by Herbert J. Brunswick, Jr.

Adam Had to Die
Hidden Truth Revealed Series
by Herbert J. Brunswick, Jr.

Printed in the United States of America

ISBN 9781629527307

All rights reserved solely by the author.
The author guarantees all contents are original and do not infringe upon the legal rights of any other person or work. No part of this book may be reproduced in any form without the permission of the author. The views expressed in this book are not necessarily those of the publisher.

Unless otherwise indicated,
Bible quotations are taken from the
Authorized King James Version of the Bible.

www.xulonpress.com

Contents

In the Beginning 11

How God Made Man 17

Definitions 21

The Image of God 27

Be Fruitful and Multiply 35

Why Was the Tree of Knowledge Placed in the
    Garden 45

Made in the Image of Christ 53

Teaching That Makes Sense

Foreword

All my life I was taught that Adam and Eve were born on the same day. I never realized the importance of why God made man first, then woman. This book revealed to me why God made man the way He did, in His own image. The explanation of the purpose of removing a rib from man to form woman opened my eyes to what it actually symbolized.

The author makes a comparison to man's makeup to that of a seed. This enabled me to relate the purpose behind why God created man in His image. Christ himself came from God, just as woman came from man.

As I read further, it all began to make sense how sin produced death, making it necessary for reproduction to occur.

This book showed me the spiritual and, above all, the physical change that took place with their bodies once they disobeyed God's commandment. The author explained all too well the purpose of why something had to happen to make death imminent, thus allowing Adam and Eve to be fruitful and multiply. By reading this book, I was able to understand the process of the transformation from the natural body to the spiritual body and my being made in the image of God. Understanding all these principles and the order of God's Divine purpose will help you to understand why Adam had to die.

Terry W. Scott

"We are of God: he that knoweth God heareth us: he that is not of God heareth not us. Hereby know we the spirit of truth, and the spirit of error." (1 John 4:6)

In the Beginning

In the beginning when God made man, He formed man from the dust of the ground, and breathed into his nostrils the breath of life, and man *became* something. What did man become? He *became* a living soul (Genesis 2:7). Therefore, the ingredients for making man were:

Dust of the ground + Breath of life = Man
(a living soul).

The soul does not exist without the combination of the *breath of life* and the *dust of the ground*. Contrary to popular teachings, man does not have a spirit that lives in a body and also *possesses* a soul. No! *Man is a soul*. He is a "living soul." First Corinthians 15:45 confirms this. It reads, "And the first man Adam was *made a living soul*." So, if there is a living soul, then, can there be a dead soul? Can the soul die? Yes! And, some will die twice.

Traditional teachings teach that when we die, our soul lives forever. They teach that if you are saved, your soul goes to heaven; and, if you are not saved, your soul goes to hell. This is partially true. But, this truth is time-dependent. This does not happen until after the resurrection, not after the first death. Let me explain. If you are saved, the soul that is recreated after the resurrection (born again) will be made up of the breath of life (spirit of God) and an *incorruptible body*. That soul will live forever. But, this is not true for those who are not saved. Ezekiel 18:20 says, "The soul that sinneth, it shall die." Also read Ezekiel 18:4-9 and James 5:20.

Now, how can Ezekiel 18:20 say that "The soul that sinneth, it shall die?" Didn't Ezekiel know that everybody is going to die? One of the most challenging issues Christ had was in His attempt to explain the difference between the first death (sleep) and the second death (the lake of fire). Virtually everyone will experience the first death, and everyone will be resurrected from the dead some day.

> Marvel not at this: for the hour is coming, in the which *all* that are in the graves shall hear his voice, And shall come forth; they that have *done good*, unto the *resurrection of life*; and they that have *done evil*, unto the *resurrection of damnation*. (John 5:28-29)

So, when Ezekiel says, "The soul that sinneth, it shall die," Ezekiel was actually talking about the second death, not the first death which Christ described as sleep.

In the Beginning

The apostles also called this first death "sleep." An example of this is found in 1 Corinthians 15:51-53:

> Behold, I show you a mystery; We shall not all *sleep*, but we shall all be changed, In a moment, in the twinkling of an eye, at the last trump: for the trumpet shall sound, and *the dead shall be raised incorruptible*, and we shall be changed. For this corruptible must *put on incorruption*, and this mortal must put on immortality.

Also read John 11:11-14 to see what Christ said concerning the death of Lazarus. Christ tried to explain to everyone that Lazarus was asleep, but they just couldn't understand it.

Another example is in Luke 8:52-55 where Christ raised a young girl from death:

> Weep not *she is not dead, but sleepeth*. And they laughed him to scorn, knowing that she was dead. And he put them all out, and took her by the hand, and called, saying, Maid, arise. And *her spirit came again*, and she arose straightway: and he commanded to give her meat.

So, when Christ said in John 8:51, "If a man keep my saying, he shall never see death," He was not talking about the first death that He calls sleep.

He was talking about the second death that is the lake of fire. The death that will cause that soul to die is the second death. It is at the second death where there is no more resurrection. Revelation 20:6 reads, "Blessed and holy is he that hath part in the first resurrection: on such the second death hath no power." This second death is where "the soul that sinneth, it shall die" when it is thrown into the lake of fire (Revelation 20:12-15).

Christ said that anyone who hears His word and believes on God shall pass from death (sleep) unto life. In other words, they will be awakened out of their sleep when their spirit returns at the resurrection into eternal life. John 5:24 reads, "Verily, verily, I say unto you, He that heareth my word, and believeth on him that sent me, hath everlasting life, and shall not come into condemnation; but is *passed from death unto life*." Tradition teaches that when you die (sleep) you immediately go to heaven to live with God. That does not appear to be what the Bible teaches. It teaches that the spirit of man goes back to God, but the body goes back to the earth. James 2:26 says, "For as the body without the spirit is dead, so faith without works is dead also." People who suggest that the spirit and the soul are one in the same appears to be teaching doctrine rather than Scripture.

Again, let's read what John 5:28-29 says. It reads, "Marvel not at this: for the hour is coming, in the which all that are in the graves shall hear his voice, And shall come forth; they that have **done** good, unto the resurrection of life; and they that have **done** evil, unto the resurrection of damnation." Now, how can

In the Beginning

you be in heaven and in the grave at the same time? You can do it because your spirit goes back to God who gave it, and your body goes back to the dust of the earth. But, when that happens, are you conscious of where you are? Ecclesiastes 9:5 says, "For the living know that they shall die: but *the dead know not any thing*, neither have they any more a reward; *for the memory of them is forgotten*." So, it is at the resurrection that the spirit reenters the body to make the **soul alive again**, as you saw demonstrated with the resurrection of the little girl in Luke 8:52-55. However, she was not resurrected in her incorruptible body.

So, as we see in the book of Acts, the patriarch David, the man who the Bible described as being after God's own heart, is dead and still buried.

Men and brethren, let me freely speak unto you of the patriarch *David, that he is both dead and buried, and his sepulchre is with us unto this day*. Therefore being a prophet, and knowing that God had sworn with an oath to him, that of the fruit of his loins, according to the flesh, he would raise up Christ to sit on his throne; He seeing this before spake of the resurrection of Christ, that his soul was not left in hell, neither his flesh did see corruption. This Jesus hath God raised up, whereof we all are witnesses. Therefore being by the right hand of God exalted, and having received of the Father the promise of the Holy Ghost, he hath shed forth this, which ye now see and hear. For **David is not ascended into the heavens**: but he saith himself, The Lord said unto my Lord, Sit thou on my right hand. (Acts 2:29-34)

So, if David, a man after God's own heart has not ascended into heaven, then why is everybody, whose funeral you have gone to, in heaven with God today?

How God Made Man

When God made man, God told man to be fruitful and multiply and replenish the earth (Genesis 1:28). As we study the Bible, we find no evidence that man fulfilled those instructions until after man sinned. Adam and Eve did not reproduce and have children until after they sinned and death was imminent. Why? Why did they not fulfill those instructions until after they sinned? Because, one of God's Divine Laws is, unless a seed dies, unless death is imminent, it cannot bear fruit. In other words, Adam had to die in order to bear fruit. Let's see how God made it possible for death to be imminent so that Adam and Eve could be fruitful and multiply.

God placed two unique trees in the garden He created for man. One of the trees was the *Tree of Life*, and the other one was the *Tree of Knowledge of Good and Evil* (Genesis 2:9). In Genesis 2:17, God commanded Adam not to eat from the Tree of Knowledge of Good and Evil. He told Adam that in the day you eat from this tree, you will surely die. In other words, you will no longer be a living soul, but you will become a dead soul. It is obvious that a dead soul is the opposite of a living soul. Ecclesiastes 12:7 tells how this is made possible. It reads, "Then shall the *dust return to the earth* as it was: and the *spirit shall return unto God* who gave it." Therefore, the formula for a dead soul, at the first death, is

Dust of the ground – Breath of life = a dead soul.

In other words, the spirit of God (or the breath of life) departs from the dust of the ground, which causes the soul not to exist until the resurrection.

As we study how God made man on day six, we see that woman is not mentioned until Genesis 2:22. In verse 23, she was called "woman" because she was *taken out of* "man." As we go back to creation week, we find in Genesis 1:26-31 that God made man on day six. I know that this might be a big surprise to you, but woman was not made on day six. After a period of time, we find in **Genesis 2:18** that God declared that it was not good that man should be alone and that He will make man a "help meet." In verse 21, we see where God caused a deep sleep to fall upon Adam, and God took a rib from Adam to make woman. After God made woman, God "... closed up the flesh *instead* thereof." This was not done on day six.

When we read Genesis 2:21 where it says "... closed up the flesh *instead* thereof," what have you been taught that this means? The question probably should be, "Has anyone taught you or has God revealed to you the deep meaning of this statement?" It is a true mystery. Naturally the human mind draws

How God Made Man

a picture of how God performed this surgery. Because many of us do not know the root meaning of certain words, we therefore interpret things from our current knowledge base. Because of it, doctrines are established that have little or nothing to do with the true information Scripture is trying to convey. Traditional teachings teach that God closed up the flesh of Adam and/or the woman after the surgery. But, hopefully you will see that this is not the total picture of what the Scripture is saying.

We must really take our time here to look at as much supporting evidence as possible to help better understand what is really happening in the beginning. It is not enough that I make statements about what is really happening without providing you with the evidence to back it up. Therefore, I will provide you with Scriptural references as well as definitions of certain root meanings of words from authoritative sources, which many of you put your trust in, so that you cannot accuse me of making things up.

On the surface, it appears that God actually took one of Adam's ribs from his body to form woman. Here is a question that might surprise you. The question is, "Did God really take a rib from Adam's body, as we all know it to be, or did God take something else that is also defined as a rib?" Another question is, "Why didn't God form the woman the same way and at the same time He formed the man?" In other words, why did God form man, then put him to sleep, and then take something out of man to make woman if He created woman at the same time and on the same day? Was that an oversight or afterthought on God's part? Was it necessary for God to remove something from man in order to make woman? If God took a rib from Adam, then what was the significance of taking a rib? Why a rib? What was the purpose for removing something from man? Was it symbolic for something? Was it because God just wanted the woman to have something that came from the man so he could say, "... bone of my bones, and flesh of my flesh?" To answer those questions, we need to dissect, break down, Genesis 2:21 by looking at the root definition of some of those words.

Definitions

Before we look at the root definition of some words, let's take a look at Genesis 2:21 again. It reads, "And the Lord God caused a deep sleep to fall upon Adam, and he slept: and he took one of his ribs, and closed up the flesh *instead* thereof." I ask the question again, why didn't God form woman the same way He formed man from the dust of the ground, side by side, at the same time He formed man? Did God close up the flesh of Adam or was it the flesh of the woman that contained Adam's rib? Did God form the other ribs in the woman to match the one He took from Adam? What was the significance of a rib?

Please pay close attention to how the Scripture reads in Genesis 2:21. It reads, "*instead* thereof." What does the words "instead thereof" mean? What is the relationship between the word "thereof" and the word "instead?" Why was the word "instead" used with the word "thereof" in this verse? It seems like it is misplaced according to our modern-day use of the word "instead." Is it used as an adverb or an adjective? Normally when we use the word "instead," we use it as an adverb. And, you would normally see it used along with the word "of" to indicate alternative, and not with the word "thereof" which indicates location. If it was used to show alternative, then, this sentence might read, "... and closed up the flesh *instead of* leaving it opened." However, the word "instead" is not used as an adverb in Genesis 2:21, but as an adjective, describing the location of the part of the flesh that was closed. So, the location where the flesh was closed is where the rib was placed to form woman.

Let's take a look at some of the root definitions of some of the words used in this verse. I realize that many of you who read this will not have access to reference material like the Strong's Exhaustive Concordance or Strong's Dictionary. So, in order to better understand what the Scriptures are conveying, it is necessary to include as much reference material as possible, thus providing as much evidence as possible. In Strong's concordance, you will find that the reference number for the word "rib" is H6763. One of the definitions for the word "rib" is "chamber." We must ask ourselves, which of the two words "rib" or "chamber" gives a better modern-day description of what Genesis 2:21 is describing? In order to make that determination, the next thing we have to do is define the word "chamber."

One of the definitions for the word "chamber" in Webster's New World Dictionary is "an *enclosed space in the body of a* plant or *animal*." When we use the word "chamber" instead of "rib," will this make more sense why God removed a "chamber" from man to make woman rather than removing a "rib?" In other words, instead of Genesis 2:21 reading "and he

Definitions

took one of his *ribs*," would you understand it better if it were to read, "... and He took one of his *chambers from his body*?" Hang in there, folks. You will begin to see the full picture as we go. But, first, we need to identify what this chamber (enclosed space) is. It was not the stomach or the intestine, but it was another chamber that was totally removed from Adam's body and placed into the dust of the ground to form the woman.

Now, let's go back to Strong's concordance to define the word "instead." The Strong's concordance number for the word "instead" is H8478. The concordance defines the word "instead" to mean "bottom (as depressed)" or "below." So, as we re-read Genesis 2:21 by using the root meanings of the words, it reads, "and He took one of his *chambers from his body* and closed up the flesh **bottom** thereof." Are you beginning to see the picture now? One of the unique things about a chamber is that it has an opening. But, God closed the entrance to the chamber He placed inside the woman. This is very important, and only the beginning of showing the mystery of how God made man and woman.

> And God said, Let us make man in our image, after our likeness: and let them have dominion over the fish of the sea, and over the fowl of the air, and over the cattle, and over all the earth, and over every creeping thing that creepeth upon the earth. So *God created man* in his own image, in the image of God created he him; male and female created he them. (Genesis 1:26-27)

Adam Had to Die

Now, let's go to Genesis 1:26-28 and Genesis 5:1 to get an even better understanding of how God made man.

In Genesis 1:27, we see that God created man. Most people, and some translations, suggest that Genesis 1:27 and Genesis 5:1 mean that God created mankind, meaning man and woman. I pray that I can break this down for you so that it is absolutely clear what is happening here. The Bible is not teaching that God created mankind or that God created man and woman at the same time on day six. You see, God created male and female inside of man on day six. And, male and female does not mean man and woman. Yes, a man is male, and a woman is female. But, male and female also describes the sex of any plant or animal. The Strong's concordance number for *male* is H2145 and the number for *man* is H120. On the other hand, the Strong's concordance number for *female* is H5347 whereas the number for *woman and wife* is H802. So, when the Bible talks about male and female, it is not just describing man and woman; but it is describing sexual components. Male and female are also words used to describe the sexual makeup of animals. The words man and woman are never used to describe animals. Man and woman are male and female, respectively. But, the words male and female do not necessarily mean man and woman as much as it is describing sexual natures. Therefore, the emphasis in using the terms male and female is about the sexual component rather than physical frame. Genesis 1:27 says that God created man "male and female," and not that God created

Definitions

man and woman. So, the Bible is talking about God creating man, not mankind. And that man was called Adam. And, Adam was made up of both male and female components inside of him, like a seed, like God—all encompassing.

Now, I know that this may be totally confusing to many of you because of what you have been taught all of these years. But, unlike Christ who spoke in parables so that only those whom God chose would understand what He was teaching, I'm not intentionally writing this so that you will not understand it. However, I do recognize that only God is able to open the eyes of those whom He has chosen to see this (Mark 4:11-12), and to understand why it is important for us to know this.

The Bible tells us that on day six, God made man. He didn't make mankind. Nor did He make man and woman. He made man, period. And that man was called Adam. Genesis 1:27 also says that God created man. This man was made to contain male and female sexual components on day six for the purpose of creating man in God's image.

The Image of God

The Bible also tells us that God created man in His image. Genesis 1:27 explains how God created man in His image. Now, before we can fully understand how God created man in His image, we need to first understand what the image of God is.

I know you have been taught the same things I was taught: that we (man) was made in the image of God because (1) we have a spirit, (2) we live in a body, and (3) we possess a soul. This was the explanation we got as ministers tried to explain how man was made in the image of God. The challenge ministers faced was, how do you compare the makeup of man with the makeup of God, (1) the Father, (2) the Son, and (3) the Holy Spirit? The only answer they could come up with was that man possessed a soul, making the soul the third component. So, they had the dust of the earth, the breath of life, and the soul as the components that makeup man. No other answer was revealed to them from Scripture. This perhaps is the root cause for the doctrine that teaches, when you die, you don't really die because the other you (your soul), that which lives inside of you, lives on after the big you dies. But, the soul is not a little you that lives inside the big you. As we studied earlier, the makeup of a soul is

**Dust of the ground + Breath of life,
the spirit of God = a soul.**

Do you know that the Bible teaches that God has a soul? When God was speaking to Moses about the things to tell the children of Israel concerning the setting up of His tabernacle with them, Leviticus 26:11 tells us, "And I will set my tabernacle among you: and *my soul* shall not abhor you." Also read Leviticus 26:30. What soul does God have? If the soul of man is composed of the dust of the ground and the breath of life, then where did God get a soul? The Bible tells us in John 4:24 that "*God is a Spirit ...*" So, how can this be? To understand how God has a soul, you will begin to fully understand how man was made in the image of God.

There are two Scripture references that illustrate how God has a soul and how we are made in the likeness of God.

But if our gospel be hid, it is hid to them that are lost: In whom the god of this world hath blinded the minds of them which believe not, lest the light of the glorious gospel of *Christ, who is the image of God*, should shine unto them." (2 Corinthians 4:3-5)

The Image of God

Who hath delivered us from the power of darkness, and hath translated us into the kingdom of his dear *Son*: In whom we have redemption through his blood, even the forgiveness of sins: *Who is the image of the invisible God*, the firstborn of every creature: For *by him were all things created, that are in heaven, and that are in earth, visible and invisible*, whether they be thrones, or dominions, or principalities, or powers: all things were created by him, and for him: And he is before all things, and by him all things consist. (Colossians 1:13-17)

In both Scripture passages, we see that Christ is "the image of God." So, God was saying in Genesis 1:26-27 that He will make man in His image. God's image is Christ. Therefore, man is to be made in the image of Christ. Now, if we believe that Christ is also God, and Christ was also made in the form of a man, then we should understand how God has a soul. As we look at the makeup of God, the Father, the Son, and the Holy Spirit, we see that the soul of God is Christ (the Son), who is the tangible, physical image of the invisible God. So then, how does this compare to the makeup of man who became a living soul like Christ?

When God made man, He created man all-in-one, like a seed, all encompassing, with both male and female components. Christ explained a similar relationship He had with God in **John 10:30**. Christ said, "I and my Father are one." Did Christ mean that figuratively or literally? When God made man, man was one, male and female, like God and Christ. In that one flesh, God made man to include both male and female components except for the organs that were needed to cleave to each other after they were separated and sin entered. There was no need for those organs that cleave together to appear outside of the body at that time because they were one flesh, like a seed. Those organs used to cleave to one another were manifested after sin entered and man's body changed to a corruptible body, a body that could die. After man's body changed in the twinkling of an eye into a corruptible body, Adam and Eve tried to hide those new organs they saw, that they then needed to cleave to one another. Adam and Eve tried to hide those newly exposed organs with fig leaves. So, when God made Adam, Adam contained all of the components of male and female (X and Y chromosomes), all wrapped up into one shell like a seed until God took the female component out of man to make woman. And, Adam's seed remained in him.

When Christ was preparing to die, He prayed in John 17:5, "And now, O Father, Glorify thou me with thine own self with the *glory which I had with thee before the world was*." How did God glorify Christ with the same glory He had with God before the world was? Christ answers this question as He continued to pray in John 17:8 by saying, "For I have given unto them the words which thou gavest me, and they have received them, and have known surely that *I came out from thee* ..." So, we see that Christ was glorified in God because He came out from God and became the soul of God, the tangible living image of God. Also, we find this declaration of Christ coming out

The Image of God

---

from God in John 16:27-28. It reads, "For the Father himself loveth you, because ye have loved me, and have believed that *I came out from God. I came forth from the Father*, and am come into the world: *again*, I leave the world, and go to the Father."

We just read in Colossians 1:16 that by Christ were all things created that are in heaven, and that are in earth, visible and invisible. This same Christ shared the *glory of God* before the world was *because Christ came out from God*, the same as the *woman came out from man*. This is one of the ways man was made in the image of God. Man was one, male and female, like God and Christ is one. As Christ came out from God, so did the female part of man came out of man to make woman. This was not a rib as we know it. It was the female chamber that was in man that God removed from man to build woman. Therefore, it was necessary for God to take one of man's ribs (the enclosed space from his body known as a womb) to make woman, thus causing the **wo**mb **man** to come out from man the way Christ came out from God, manifesting the image of God. First Corinthians 11:7-9 shows a similar comparison of the *glory of man* and his relationship with **womb man**, similar to the relationship Christ has with God. It reads, "For a man indeed ought not to cover his head, forasmuch as *he is the image and glory of God*, but *the woman is the glory of the man*. For the man is not of the woman, but *the woman of the man*. Neither was the man created for the woman, but *the woman for the man*."

Adam Had to Die

In Genesis 1:26-28 and Genesis 5:1 the Bible says that God created He *him, male and female* created He *them*. Let me try to explain what those verses are saying in a different way. Those verses are saying that God created man (*him*). There is no mention of God creating *her*. God created *him*. In the process of God creating man (*him*), God also created man (*them*). In other words, "them," male and female, were made inside of "him." God created man (male and female, *them*). The confusion is, we all have been taught and believed that God created man and woman (mankind) on day six. No! God did not create man and woman at this point. He created man to contain both male and female sexual components within man. God made one person, man. Then God totally removed the female component out of man to make woman later.

If any of you have studied biology before, you may remember that the man determines the sex of the offspring because a man has both X and Y chromosomes within him. When God created man, God made man to contain both X and Y chromosomes, male and female chromosomes. A woman has two X chromosomes in her. So, when it came time to make woman, God took the female chamber, the **wo**mb of the **man**, and placed it inside the dust of the earth to make woman, and closed the "bottom" of the **womb man** thereof. So, man and woman were still not able to reproduce at that time because the entrance of the chamber of the woman was closed, and the organ man needed to cleave remained inside of man until sin entered and death became imminent.

The Image of God

Let's go to Genesis 5:1. Perhaps it can help clear things up a little bit.

This is the book of the generations of Adam. In the day that God created man, in the likeness of God made he him; Male and female created he them; and blessed them, *and called their name Adam*, in the day when they were created. (Genesis 5:1))

Did you get that folks? God called "their name" Adam. Woman was not given a name until after they ate from the Tree of Knowledge. And, Adam is the one who named her Eve. So, at the time God created man, God called their (plural) name (singular) Adam (singular). God called them (male and female, not man and woman) by one name. He called *their name* Adam. Why, because God made one man, one person on day six. And, He made that one man in His image, because God is one. And, woman came out of man like Christ came out of God. One man, one name, having both male and female chromosomes, male and female sexual organs inside of him! God had not made woman "... in the day that God created man, in the likeness of God...."

Be Fruitful and Multiply

Ever since I was a kid, I always wondered why God placed the Tree of Knowledge of Good and Evil in the garden in the first place. I never could understand the traditional teachings that God placed the Tree of Knowledge in the garden because God loved man so much that He wanted to give man a choice between Him and Satan. I just couldn't buy that explanation, especially when no concrete evidence was given. If the answer to why God placed the Tree of Knowledge in the garden was because God loved man so much that He wanted to give man the ability to choose, then, my next question is, why was death linked to that choice? That is almost like a man telling his wife that I love you so much, therefore, I want you to have a choice between me and another man so you can prove your love for me. But, if you choose another man, then I'm going to kill you. Is that what's being insinuated here, as to why God placed the Tree of Knowledge in the garden and commanded man not to eat from it? Couldn't God have given man choices without man having to die because of it? Didn't man have the ability to choose from among the other trees in the garden? So, why was death such a significant factor in this particular choice? Did death really serve some other purpose other than what you have been taught? I thank God that He has revealed the answer to those questions that I've pondered over for a very, very long time. The challenge now is, how do I share this most difficult mystery with you so that you can understand it, too?

The Bible tells us that Adam and his wife were naked and not ashamed (Genesis 2:25). Why were they not ashamed? They were not ashamed because, the bottom of the woman's womb was closed (Genesis 2:21). And, when God made man who possessed both male and female components, man did not need an instrument to cleave to a wife at that time. Therefore, there were virtually no distinguishing features between them. Even today, men have what we call "nipples" on their chest that appear to serve no apparent purpose. Why? I know of no other male animal made that way. Why? So, Adam and his wife's body probably looked very much alike. There was no shame in their nakedness until their bodies changed, in the twinkling of an eye, and they saw something. They saw something new appearing on their new, corruptible bodies after they disobeyed God's commandment.

What happened when they ate from the Tree of Knowledge? Genesis 3:5, 7 suggest that their eyes were not opened until after they ate from the Tree of Knowledge. What do you think the Bible is referring to when it says that their eyes were opened?

Be Fruitful and Multiply

Please stay with me. Another mystery is about to be revealed.

God placed all kinds of trees in the garden for man to eat to sustain life, even to sustain eternal life. At the center of the garden He placed the Tree of Life. If man would have eaten from the Tree of Life he could have lived forever (Genesis 3:22). Also in the midst of the garden was the Tree of *Knowledge* of Good and Evil. Eating from this tree allowed man to be like God, to **know** good and evil, and to make one wise (Genesis 3:5-6).

If man had eaten from the Tree of Life, perhaps the Tree of *Knowledge* would have been removed and taken away. But, if that had happened, would man fulfill the ultimate plan of God that many would take on the image of Christ and not just Adam? I think not. Therefore, as the Bible describes the event, we see in Genesis 3:6 that the man and the woman both disobeyed the command of God and did eat from the Tree of *Knowledge,* which now allowed him to *know* his wife (Genesis 4:1) thus fulfilling the instruction to be fruitful and multiply.

In Genesis 3:7 we see that their eyes were opened, and for the first time they *knew* that they were naked. Question! Were man and woman not able to see prior to eating from the Tree of Knowledge? Genesis 3:6 says, "And when the woman *saw* that the tree was good for food, and that it was pleasant to the *eyes* ..." So, if she saw that the tree was good for food, and that it was pleasant to the eyes, I would think that she could see, wouldn't you? So, what is the Scripture talking about when it says that the "eyes" of them both were opened?

The Hebrew term for "eyes" was used in several ways not related to seeing things. We were all taught that the opening of Adam and his wife's eyes were some sort of spiritual awakening. We all knew that the man Adam and **womb man** were able to see prior to eating from the Tree of Knowledge. They were not blind. But, the mystery has been revealed that opening of their eyes were more than just a spiritual awakening and an elevated level of knowledge concerning their nakedness because they knew something they had never known or seen before. That was the knowledge of their reproductive system.This system was capable of producing good and evil.It was the components they needed to cleave together to become one again.And, it was manifested after they disobeyed the commandment of God.

For too long, this just did not make a lot of sense. How could they both see before eating from the Tree of Knowledge and not have shame in their nakedness until after they ate from it? There had to be a logical explanation for this phenomenon. I give praise and thanks to Almighty God for opening my eyes and understanding to what this verse really says.

After Adam and his wife ate from the Tree of Knowledge, Genesis 3:7 tells us, "And the *eyes* of them both were opened, and they *knew* that they were naked." Naturally, when we see the word "eyes," we immediately think about the two objects in our heads that we use for seeing. Or, again, we look at our eyes being open as some sort of spiritual awakening. But,

Be Fruitful and Multiply

the Bible did not tell us that Adam and his wife saw something when their eyes were opened. No, the Bible tells us that they *knew* something when their eyes were opened. You see, it wasn't the eyes in their heads that were opened, nor was it just a spiritual awakening of the purpose of those organs they saw. They also saw something different about themselves, as well. If it was just a spiritual manifestation, then there would not have been a need for them to cover themselves. But, this was more than a spiritual awakening. It was a physical manifestation of their new-found organs. Those organs were needed to cleave to one another in order for them to be fruitful and to multiply. It was the chamber that God had closed, and the instrument man needed to cleave to his wife, that were now opened and exposed. Because of that, they tried to hide the evidence from God with fig leaves.

Satan had told the woman earlier in Genesis 3:5 that God knew that in the day you eat from the Tree of Knowledge that your *eyes would be opened*, and you would *be as gods, knowing* something, not seeing something, but knowing something. And, the first and only *knowledge* the two seem to have gained was about their reproductive systems. How did they *know* that they were naked? They knew that they were naked because something happened to them, physically. There was a physical change in their bodies; in the twinkling of the eyes they put on this new, corruptible body. Also, why, when their eyes were opened, was their nakedness the only thing they knew? Why just their nakedness? Were there other things they could now see that they didn't see before? Why did nakedness play the central role in their eyes opening? As we study the Bible, we should always try to seek "purpose." Always ask yourself, what is the purpose?

When we look at the Strong's Exhaustive Concordance and Bible Dictionary to learn the origin and meaning of the word "eyes," we find that the number in the Strong's concordance for the word "eyes" is H5869. One of the definitions for this word "eyes" is fountain, and it is used as an analogy in (the eye of the landscape). So, we see that the fountain (the eye of man's landscape/fountain where water flows) was opened. In Adam, and in his wife's case, this is the fountain of life that is opened. Therefore, as we re-read Genesis 3:7 using the root meaning of the word, it was not talking about a spiritual awakening. No, it was talking about a physical change taking place, God exposed something that was hidden on them before they ate from the Tree of Knowledge. How was it hidden? It was hidden because when God took woman out of man, He closed up the bottom of her womb (Genesis 2:21). Man had no need for a cleaving organ at that time since the female component was originally in man, like a seed, then afterwards when God removed the womb from man, it was closed up. Why? It was closed up because God does not allow reproduction unless death is imminent. And, the only thing that produces death is sin. Further, death was not imminent for Adam and his wife until after they disobeyed God's commandment.

Now that they were no longer self-contained in one body, there was only one way for them to become one again, by man cleaving unto his wife.

Our definition of a man and woman becoming one is not the same as God's definition. We define man and woman as becoming one when a man and a woman participate in a marriage ceremony and say "I do." But, God's definition of becoming one is when a man cleaves to a woman, they then become one flesh. The Pharisees asked Christ was it lawful for a man to put away his wife. Christ answered and said in Matthew 19:4-**6:**

Have ye not read that he which made them at the beginning made them male and female, And said, For this cause shall a man leave father and mother, and *shall cleave to his wife: and they twain shall be one flesh? Wherefore they are no more twain, but one flesh.*)

Again, this applies to a man who cleaves to any woman. In 1 Corinthians 6:16, the Bible reads, "What? know ye not that he which is joined to an harlot is one body? for two, saith he, *shall be* one flesh." The Bible uses this same analogy to describe Christ and the church.

For we are members of his body, of his flesh, and of his bones. For this cause shall a man leave his father and mother, and *shall be* joined unto his wife, and they two *shall be* one flesh. This is a great mystery: but I speak concerning Christ and the church. (Ephesians 5:30-32))

We must be careful how we interpret the words fornication and adultery when reading the Bible because it may be describing your relationship with Christ; and not your relationship with a man or woman. Paul wrote to the Corinthian church telling them in 2 Corinthians 11:2, "... for I have espoused you to one husband, that I may present you as a chaste virgin to Christ." Also read Revelation 14:4.

So, Adam prophesied about how he and his wife would become one again in Genesis 2:24. It reads, "Therefore *shall* a man leave his father and his mother, and *shall cleave* unto his wife: and they *shall* be one flesh." But, in order for Adam and his wife to become one flesh again, something had to occur to manifest the organs needed for cleavage. Their "eyes" (the fountain where life flows) of the chamber had to be opened. Therefore, copulation was not possible until their eyes were opened. To be fruitful and to multiply was not possible until *death entered*. And, death was not possible until *sin entered*. Now, we are getting closer to the reason the Tree of Knowledge was placed in the garden in the first place. We will study more about this later.

We also find the Strong's concordance number H5869 for the word "eyes" is also used for the word "fountain" in Genesis 16:7 and Numbers 33:9.

> And the angel of the LORD found her by a *fountain* of water in the wilderness, by the fountain in the way to Shur. (Genesis 16:7)

Be Fruitful and Multiply

> And they removed from Marah, and came unto Elim: and in Elim were twelve fountains of water, and threescore and ten palm trees; and they pitched there. (Numbers 33:9)

So, again, evidence from an authoritative source showing that the same Hebrew word for the word "eyes" is also used for the word "fountain," having similar meanings.

It was not until after Adam and his wife ate from the Tree of Knowledge that Adam named his wife Eve. There was a purpose for Adam naming her Eve. The Bible tells us she was named Eve because she became the mother of all living. But, how did she become the mother of all living? Because of what she had done that caused the reproductive process to begin, to be fruitful and to multiply (Genesis 3:20). Eve evolved from female to woman, and then from woman to Eve. Also, it was not until Adam and his wife ate from the Tree of Knowledge that Adam and Eve were able to copulate. After Eve ate from the Tree of Knowledge, God handed down His sentence to her. Genesis 3:16 reads, "Unto the woman he said, I will greatly multiply thy sorrow and thy conception; *in sorrow thou shalt bring forth children; and thy desire shall be to thy husband, and he shall rule over thee.*"

Question! Did Eve experience sorrow before eating from the Tree of Knowledge? The answer to that question is, no. Then, if Eve did not experience sorrow prior to eating from the Tree of Knowledge, then how could God increase what she didn't already have? The emphasis here is not to increase an existing situation, but that the situation (sorrow she would experience in pregnancy and childbirth) would exceed all of the other sorrows she will have. The Bible is specific and clear about what Eve's sorrow would be. God proceeded by saying specifically, "*in sorrow* thou shalt bring forth children."

Second question! Does the Bible show where Eve had children before they ate from the Tree of Knowledge? Neither Adam nor Eve was able to bring forth children before they ate from the Tree of Knowledge. It was not until Genesis 4:1 where we see anything about Eve having children. Adam did not know his wife, in a biblical sense, until God opened their "eyes" and they *knew* they were naked, the channel to reproduction. Genesis 4:1 reads, "And Adam *knew* Eve his wife; and she conceived, and bare Cain, and said, I have gotten a man from the LORD." Genesis 3:16 also said, "and *thy desire shall be to thy husband*." Eve's desire was not to her husband until after they ate from the Tree of Knowledge. I'm not going to elaborate on the third sentence God handed down to Eve, only because I don't think it is that essential to this lesson. But, eating from the Tree of *Knowledge* granted Adam the ability to *know* his wife to the degree that they became fruitful and multiplied (Genesis 4:1).

Why was the Tree of Knowledge placed in the Garden?

I didn't know why God placed the Tree of Knowledge in the garden, so I accepted what appeared to be the most logical answer man could give at that time. But, deep down inside, I knew there had to be a real biblical answer to this question. Not only did there have to be a real biblical answer, but that answer had to make sense.

I knew that there had to be a very good reason for God to place a tree in the garden and command man not to eat from it, other than to give man a choice. God did give man a choice, however. But, the choice was between life and death, prosperity and poverty, joy and pain (sorrow), good and evil. You might ask, did God create evil? Isaiah 45:7 says so. It reads, "I form the light, and create darkness: I make peace, and *create evil*: I the LORD do all these things." Therefore, man could not have experienced death, sorrow, and evil unless *sin entered* into the picture. And, how was *sin entered* into the picture? It was entered when Adam and his wife disobeyed God's *law*. Where there is no law, there can be no transgression (Roman 4:15). The law that *entered* was the commandment "You should not eat from the Tree of Knowledge of Good and Evil." God asked Adam in Genesis 3:11, "Hast thou eaten of the tree, whereof *I commanded thee* that thou shouldest not eat?"

Sin entered by the law that caused death. And, when death entered, that initiated the process by which man could multiple and replenish the earth. Romans 5:12 reads, "Wherefore, as by one man *sin entered* into the world, and death by sin; and so death passed upon all men, for that all have sinned:" And, as we read further, we find in Romans 5:20, "Moreover the *law entered, that the offence might abound* ..."

You are probably asking the question, "Is the Bible telling us in Romans 5:20 that God placed the Tree of Knowledge in the garden and entered a law not to eat from it so that man could sin?" Please stay with me. I want the Scriptures to answer these questions for you. In order to do so, we must answer the question, "What offense was abounded?"

The Strong's number for the word "abound" is G4121. The popular translation of this word is to "increase." However, there are two other meanings of the word "abound" that we seem to ignore when reading this verse. Those words are in the form of the verbs "to do" and "to make." In other words, they mean "to occur" or "to make happen." Therefore, the law was entered that the offense might occur. But, we still have not answered what offense Romans 5:20 is referring to.

We need not go far to identify what offense Romans 5:20 is referring to. The answer is between Romans 5:12 that talks about *sin entering*, and Romans 5:20 that talks about the *law entering*. Let's look at each occurrence of the word "offense" to understand what offense Romans 5:20 is referring to.

- **Romans 5:15**: "But not as the *offence*, so also is the free gift. For if through the *offence of one many be dead*, much more the grace of God, and the gift by grace, which is by one man, Jesus Christ, hath abounded unto many."
- **Romans 5:16**: "And not as it was by *one that sinned*, so is the gift: for the judgment was by one to condemnation, but the free gift is of many offences unto justification."
- **Romans 5:17**: "For if *by one man's offence death reigned* by one; much more they which receive abundance of grace and of the gift of righteousness shall reign in life by one, Jesus Christ."
- **Romans 5:18**: "Therefore as *by the offence of one* judgment came upon all men to condemnation; even so by the righteousness of one the free gift came upon all men unto justification of life."

We see from the context of these verses that the offense in Romans 5:20 is referring to the offense of Adam that is continually described in verses

15-18. The Bible says in Romans 5:20 that the law (thou shall not eat from the Tree of Knowledge) was entered so that the offense of Adam might occur. So, why was it necessary for this offense to occur?

Have you ever noticed the longevity of a seed? If a seed is not exposed to the elements that cause germination and growth, like moisture and sun light, a seed will just lay there forever. But, as soon as it is planted (dies), that activates the process to become fruitful. So was the case with Adam. Adam was born of God. He had all of the components needed for reproduction contained within him, like a seed. But, unlike a seed, Adam could not die because he was born of God and in the image of God. The only thing that could activate death is sin. Therefore, God had to expose Adam to an environment that would initiate death in order for Adam to die and to be fruitful and multiply. **Romans 6:23** says, "For the wages of sin is death." And the only thing that could have caused sin was the disobedience of a law. First Corinthians 15:56 says, "The sting of death is sin; and the strength of sin is the law." Which law caused the death of Adam and Eve? It was the law that commanded them not to eat from the Tree of Knowledge. Therefore, Adam had to have the opportunity to sin in order for him to die. And, without sin, Adam would not have been able to reproduce, to fulfill one of God's divine plans for man to be fruitful and to multiply.

But, was being fruitful and to multiply the only objective in God's divine plan? No, there is more to God's plan than being fruitful and multiplying.

Why was the Tree of Knowledge placed in the Garden?

Ephesians 1:4-5 tells us that God had chosen *us in Christ* before the foundation of the world.

According as *he hath chosen us in him before the foundation of the world*, that we should be holy and without blame before him in love: *Having predestinated us unto the adoption of children by Jesus Christ to himself, according to the good pleasure of his will.* (Ephesians 1:4-5)

So, if God had predestinated us (plural) in Christ before the foundation of the world, then Adam had to die in order for us to need a savior, to be in Christ. As God made provisions for man to be fruitful and to multiply, He also made provision for man to be reconciled back to Him through Christ. Psalm 90:3 says, "Thou turnest man to destruction; and sayest, Return, ye children of men."

Not only did Adam have to die, but was it also necessary for Christ to die? Christ declared in John 12:24, just as He was preparing for His death, "Verily, verily, I say unto you, *Except a corn of wheat fall into the ground and die, it abideth alone*: but if it die, it bringeth forth much fruit." I submit unto you that the reason God placed the Tree of Knowledge in the Garden of Eden, and then commanded man not to eat from it, was so man would not abide alone and so that man could be fruitful to fulfill God's divine plan, for us to be in Christ, made in His image. So, how would God's divine plan for us in Christ be fulfilled?

As we read earlier, God made man in His image. When God made man, death was not imminent. First John 3:9 tells us, "Whosoever is born of God doth not commit sin; for *his seed remaineth in him*: and he cannot sin, because he is born of God." Before God made woman, Adam's seed remained in him. He was all encompassing. Everything was in one body. Since his seed remained in him, he could not die. Because he could not die, he was also unable to reproduce until sin entered. Sin could not enter until there was a law for Adam to transgress. That law was, "Do not eat from the Tree of Knowledge."

So, just like Christ stated, unless a seed dies, it abides alone and cannot bear fruit. Therefore, God provided an environment that would prevent man from abiding alone because Adam's seed remained in him. Genesis 2:18 reads, "And the LORD God said, It is not good that the man should *be alone*; I will make him an help meet for him." So, God made woman by putting Adam to sleep, then removed the female chamber out of man to make woman.

When God made woman, that provided the avenue by which Adam's seed would not remain in him. But, even then, death still was not imminent. Something had to occur to make death imminent. And, Adam's seed still remained in him because their "eyes" (the fountain at the center of their landscape where life flows) were not opened. Therefore, God set up the environment that could cause death, thus opening up man and woman's fountains for man's seed to leave him and be planted in the earth called woman, to be fruitful and to multiply. This was the purpose for the Tree of Knowledge being placed in the garden, and God commanding man not to eat from it, so that the offense might occur. After the offense occurred, then death became imminent. And, when death became imminent, Adam and Eve were able to be fruitful and multiply, to have children that we, too, might be made in the image of Christ.

Made in the Image of Christ

So, then, what is the process for our being in Christ? First Corinthians 15 does an excellent job explaining this.

For since by man came death, by man came also the resurrection of the dead. For as in Adam all die, even so in Christ shall all be made alive. (1 Corinthians 15:21-22)

But some man will say, How are the dead raised up? and with *what body do they come*? Thou fool, *that which thou sowest is not quickened, except it die*: And that which thou sowest, *thou sowest not that body that shall be*, but bare grain, it may chance of wheat, or of some other grain: But *God giveth it a body as it hath pleased him*, and to every seed his own body. (1 Corinthians 15:35-38)

To fulfill God's divine purpose that we be in Christ, God had purposed before the foundation of the world that we have a body like Christ. You might ask, 'Why didn't God create such a body in the beginning?' Let's continue in 1 Corinthians 15.

> So also is the resurrection of the dead. It is sown in corruption; it is raised in incorruption: It is sown in dishonour; it is raised in glory: it is sown in weakness; it is raised in power: *It is sown a natural body; it is raised a spiritual body.* There is a natural body, and there is a spiritual body. And so it is written, The first man Adam was made a living soul; the last Adam was made a quickening spirit. *Howbeit that was not first which is spiritual, but that which is natural; and afterward that which is spiritual.* The first man is of the earth, earthy: the second man is the Lord from heaven. As is the earthy, such are they also that are earthy: and as is the heavenly, such are they also that are heavenly. *And as we have borne the image of the earthy, we shall also bear the image of the heavenly."* When this happens, this will consummate the process of man in Christ and our being in the image of God. (1 Corinthians 15:42-49))

After man receives his spiritual body, man becomes full circle. Man then enters back into a position by which he is not able to reproduce because he is born again of God and cannot die. The Sadducees, who did not believe in the resurrection, asked Christ a question. They asked Him, 'Who would a woman be the wife of if seven brothers took her to wife and she did not have children for any of them?' Christ explained to them that there is no reproduction after the resurrection.

> Then came to him certain of the Sadducees, which deny that there is any resurrection; and they asked him, Saying, Master, Moses wrote unto us, If any man's brother die, having a wife, and he die without children, that his brother should take his wife, and raise up seed unto his brother. There were therefore seven brethren: and the first took a wife, and died without children. And the second took her to wife, and he died childless. And the third took her; and in like manner the seven also: and they left no children, and died. Last of all the woman died also. Therefore in the resurrection whose wife of them is she? for seven had her to wife. And Jesus answering said unto them, The children of this world marry, and are given in marriage: But *they which shall be accounted worthy to obtain that world, and the resurrection from the dead, neither marry, nor are given in marriage: Neither can they die any more: for they are equal unto the angels; and are the children of God*, being the children of the resurrection. (Luke 20:27-36))

After God's divine purpose for man to multiply, replenish the earth, and we are raised in our spiritual bodies, we will no longer be able to reproduce. God's divine purpose of our being in Christ, made in His image would have been fulfilled. For God to accomplish this without breaking His physical law, "unless a seed dies it cannot bear fruit," Adam had to die. Amen!

CPSIA information can be obtained
at www.ICGtesting.com
Printed in the USA
FFOW04n0852101214